AFRICAN POETRY CHAPBOOKS ANTHOLOGY:

Vol 1

Curated and edited by:

**Tendai Rinos Mwanaka
Lorna Telma Zita
Helder Simbad**

Mwanaka Media and Publishing Pvt Ltd,
Chitungwiza Zimbabwe

Creativity, Wisdom and Beauty

Publisher: *Mmap*
Mwanaka Media and Publishing Pvt Ltd
24 Svosve Road, Zengeza 1
Chitungwiza Zimbabwe
mwanaka@yahoo.com
mwanaka13@gmail.com
www.africanbookscollective.com/publishers/mwanaka-media-and-publishing
https://facebook.com/MwanakaMediaAndPublishing/

Distributed in and outside N. America by African Books Collective
orders@africanbookscollective.com
www.africanbookscollective.com

ISBN: 978-1-77928-206-4
EAN: 9781779282064

© Tendai Rinos Mwanaka 2025

All rights reserved.
No part of this book may be reproduced or transmitted in any form or by any means, mechanical or electronic, including photocopying and recording, or be stored in any information storage or retrieval system, without written permission from the publisher

DISCLAIMER
All views expressed in this publication are those of the author and do not necessarily reflect the views of *Mmap*.

TABLE OF CONTENTS

Chapbook by Archie Swanson
to write
the bicycle
the inky black
Pelion
no Notre Dame
to be fair
silver ball
mother of three
crabs of Wexford Bridge
cheers bru
chestnut tree
fallen
tell me I lived
666
a bridge too far

....

For My Father, Now I Know... by Tendai Rinos Mwanaka
If I had known
Fishing
The Womb of Time
Mandirata

Silent journey from the East: Villages, Towns and Cities...
Memory House: I am my father's Son
God is dead?
Meal Times
Grief
The Names We Borrowed
The park
Soul
Death
Earth
Green Arcades
The river flowing
Deepening skies
Constructions
People
Love
The setting sun
Instructions
Hate
Cars, buses, lorries,
Blue hills of home
In the villages

....

Chapbook by Lorna Zita
Mãe África
O fim da dor

Mãe natureza
Viver é agora
Amores
Quando o silêncio chegar
Desabo por dentro
Ser Mulher
Saudade
O que dizer ao mar
Silêncio
Medo
Não quero ser poeta
Já não sou o mesmo
Que amanheça logo
Volta logo
....

effigies of a madman by Beaton Galafa
procession
from nowhere
rituals
in awe
broken fingers
April
Illusions
jogging
empty gourds
treading mountains
effigies

places
a lover's melody
2005
silent rocks
dosing
apotheosis
Pentecost on the hills
a season of harvest
water
cryptic
we could've come
tears
a word of departure

....

Chapbook by Mondo Kobi Arnold
Absurde absolu
Ce qui est la vie
Ce qu'elle est
A toi m'amour
Ode à la féminité
Doux soleil et belle lune
Femme de distinction
Dilection
Monde à l'envers
Le pli à elle
Ombre opaque
L'ironie du sort

Après la rupture
Nostalgie
Ma vie nouvelle
La Ballade
Espoir de l'oubli
Cantique africain
Quidam
Ma défense
....
This Traveller by Jabulani Mzinyathi
The Traveler
Stolen
Second Routing
The Investors
Trinkets
Burial Ground
Scattered
Listening
Friends Or Fiends
The Patriots
Self Preservation
The End
Gladiators
Terrible Twins
The Influences
the earth
Done And Dusted

Littered Road
The Same Crowd
Chapter Closed
The Chitutes
To My Buddy
Of Blips and Blunders
Gweru
Servant Leader

....
Chapbook by Maria Manuel G. A. de Menezes
COQUEIRO DA MINHA PRAIA
MANGAL
ZUNGUEIRAS DO MUSSULO
POR ÁFRICA
NÃO AO RACISMO
MIGRANTES
O QUE FARÁ A MINHA PROMESSA?
O PODER DE PODER
O SOM DO SILÊNCIO
CONFORMISMO? NÃO
AUSENTES NO PRESENTE
MONTE PERTO DO CÉU
STRESS ZERO
GOTA A GOTA, CLIQUE A CLIQUE
CHLOOOC... CHLUC... PLOC

....
Provoked Poems by Sebastian Jalameso

Holier-Than-Thou
The Sentence
Primitive Civilisation
The Liberated
Power Begets Power
Garden of Heroes
I Want to Hold My Political Wife
Tribal Pheromones
Song of Village Chicken
The Cross for the Grave
Why So Faint the Memory?
Parliamentary Infidelity
Dissolving in Spiritual Orgasms
Tribute to the Womb
From Libido to Creativity
A Wife on Sale
Three Wicked COVID
I Was Born an Idiot
Cow on Heat and Tickler
Song of Seventy-Seven
Ode to the Breast
Anus, the Political Maw
Cracks in God's Weld

....

APROPRIAÇÃO ERÓTICA DA ORALIDADE: CRÍTICA DO *EGO DO FOGO* NO ESPAÇO

ANTROPOLÓGICO DO MATERIALISMO FILOSÓFICO by Helder Simbad

....

Chapbook by Annette Mbapa "Diva" Ikongo
Alone with the Others
5 pounds, 8 ounces
Birdie
Tuesday
Car Rides
Writer
Nimbus
Ahoy!
Forgive Yourself
C'est Tout?
10th November
The Several Stages of Grief
Inner Light
Situationship
Different Kinds of Heartbreak
Heaven
House for Sale
The In-Between
Locked in Time

....

Os "novíssimos" e a Poética Escrita de Motivação Oral: transdução das traduções de *Raízes Cantam* e *Pintura*

dos Ecos: A palavra (de cada geração) é cara
só a vida a compra e a beija Job Sipitali
....
Nature sings by Obinna Chilekezi
Movement song
Good morning birds
For love's sake
Rainbow
Nightingale
Harmattan Dawn
Dawn
Your card arrived
An escape from
Half of the yellow sun
The melt down
Frustrated people
Walking away from bygone of you
Economic meltdown
For a new dawn
Umunama
Together as sky
Poem of dawn at dawn
Rejection
....
Mmap New African Poets Series

Preface

After running *Best New African Poets* anthologies for 10 years we have decided we are now grown ups in the poetry world, so we decided to show how mature we are to the poetry and literary world by focussing on a few poets per year now. Each poet comes in with a clutch of poems, what some call chapbooks or pamplets.

Just like with BNAP we let each poet decide what they want to address, so its a broad range of earthy issues. This is the first in yearly series of collection of chapbook by African poets. We are working with poets we have worked with for the past 10 years, maybe in the future we will open to other poets. But we don't intent for BNAP to die. It will continue as African Languages Anthology where we give space to poems written in African languages, meaning languages that were formed in Africa and spoken by Africans as their mother tongues. We want to continue preserving our languages.

This new anthology, *African Poetry Chapbooks Anthology, Vol 1* has 12 poets, with 12 chapbooks written in English, French and Portuguese chosen among poets in these countries, South Africa, Zimbabwe, Nigeria, Tanzania, Malawi, Uganda, Mozambique, Angola, Sao Tome and DRC. Enjoy !

CHAPBOOK BY ACHIE SWANSON

Bio

Archie Swanson has published five collections of poetry — *the stretching of my sky* (2018), *the shores of years* (2019), *beyond a distant edge* (2021), *of clay* (2022), and *at the estuary* (2024). A sixth book of 250 selected poems called *winnowings* will be released this year. Poems have been published in the triannual South African poetry magazines, *Stanzas* and *New Contrast*. His work has also featured in all of the *Best New African Poetry Anthologies*

(BNAP), from 2015 to 2024. Three poems translated into Spanish by poet López-Vega appeared in 2016 in the Spanish National Newspaper, *El Mundo*. In addition, his poetry has appeared in the Patricia Schonstein-curated anthologies, *Absolute Africa!* (2018) and *Naturally Africa!* (2020) and the *McGregor Poetry Festival Anthologies* (2014 and 2016-2022). In 2017 poems were shortlisted for the European Union Sol Plaatje Award and the UK Bridport Prize. His poem, 'my Guernica' placed second out of 15,000 poems in the AVBOB Poetry Competition (English/2019). He was one of four international guest poets invited to the Nigerian Abuja Writers' Forum "Poetry – Nuts and Bolts" event in August 2021. He has also collaborated regularly with celebrated composer, Grant McLachlan, with his poem 'déjà vu' being the inspiration for the composition, *from the direction it should depart*, performed at the Baxter Concert Hall in 2019. He also wrote the words, translated into isiXhosa by Lungile Ka-Nyamezela, for a choral piece entitled *Intombazana*, composed by Grant McLachlan for performance by the Herschel Chorale at the 2020 World Choir Games. Two of his poems are included in Grant McLachlan's song cycle entitled the *silence of the day* (2023), which in 2023 and 2024 was performed in the Wigmore Hall and sung by Roderick Williams (who sung at the coronation of King Charles) at St. George the Martyr church in London, and at The Ludlow English

Song   Weekend   in   Shropshire.
www.instagram.com/poetarchie

to write

gather discarded clothes
life's jetsam
vestments imbued
with hope and loss

shred to rags
stir and beat
steep
in hardwood casks

dip the deckle
into milky soup
lift gently
shake and drain

place on felt
dry on horsehair rope
use stone to smooth
each paper sheet

mix gallnut
iron vitriol
and gum of Arabic
with wine and rain

now take the quill and ink it well
and cast illuminated text
onto the textured fabric of this world

the bicycle

14.45 Friday 29 December 2023
there is an unattended bicycle
with a yellow plastic crate strapped on the back
leaning against a lamppost in front of Nasser Hospital
on El Baheer Street in Khan Younis
two men are chatting near the CNN-News18 live
webcam
an ambulance departs cautiously honking its way through
the pedestrians
visitors climb the stairwell to the right of the entrance
a boy runs past
a mother in her hijab drags two young children along
behind her

there is someone hammering in the distance

08.13 Sunday 31 December 2023
ambulance sirens wail in the distance
washing is drying in an open 2nd floor hospital window
the unattended bicycle is still leaning against the lamppost
a stream of people are walking past in both directions
a Japan International Cooperation Agency refuse truck trundles by
a man in a white shirt sneezes
wipes his nose with the palm of his hand
an IDF drone buzzes above

10.19 Sunday 25 February 2024
only the bicycle leaning against the lamppost remains

the inky black

the sleepers and the steely track
the buffer stop
no junction here or signalman
with points to divert on

no stationmaster
no baggage porter

no first class and dining car
just cattle trucks from end to end

this is the final stop
the journey's close
a single fare
no option of return

a one-way ride
a terminating train
the end of line
the end of time

the shower room
the Zyklon B
the chimney stack
the inky black

Pelion

there is a squashed sun on the risen horizon
there is a mountain with distilled streams
and a booted eagle hanging in an indigo sky
on outstretched wings
where ancient hardwood forests thrive
formed of gnarled trees

and of ancient rocks and velvet moss and bees
where spotted fauns prick timid ears
and apples and chestnuts hug tumbling slopes
where swooping swallows scoop variegated tears
from gilded sheets of mirrored dusk
and honking donkeys
call to furtive foxes in the night

here warm rains fall
from thunderous vaults
and here in the worn flag-stoned square of Tsagarada
the ancient plane has stood a thousand years

on Pelion in the Centaur's cave
Jason learnt the secrets of plants and hunting and the arts
and sailing forth to distant Colchis with his Argonauts
ploughed dragon's teeth with fire-snorting bulls to snatch
his golden fleece
past these rugged shores a thousand ships did sail
sinewed arms straining at the oars
on a morning when the shadows of hurried clouds
scurried across the buffeted sea
towards the bloodied sun of Troy

here too like a giant ray I swam
along time-sedimented cliffs
arms fanning forward

legs thrusting out
I swam and I swam through stained-glass blue
I heard the burnished pebbles rolling on the shore
I heard my glad lungs sigh
I heard my thoughts play
I heard the stretching of my sky

no Notre Dame

no Notre Dame
no slated roof
just open sky and vaults that tower heavenward

there are no bronze bells here that measure out the time
and call on me to genuflect before a gilded shrine
there are alone the ringing bells of memories sublime

no flying buttress here to hold cold stone walls up
no copper knocker here to knock
or boarded door by which to enter in

there is no aisle to take me through – no transept and no pew
nor patterned tiles to walk along

instead the paths of little duikers lead me on

no choir in the choir stall – it's here that nature sings
there is no sound of organ pipes
to drown the ocean's whisperings

there is no idol in this church
except a woodgrained gargoyle face
sandblasted by the wind

the capstones to these arches lock blocks of blue in place
the stained-glass windows of transparent hue
in place of incense shroud there's just a wisp of cirrus
cloud

this sanctuary is not enclosed
nor hidden from the view
the nave and chancel stretch as far as I can look

no patterned altar draping here
no little bell and silverware
no offering or chalice and no book

this table laid to feast upon cannot be added to
except by tiny fynbos blooms
that flower in the spring

to be fair

Aussie! Aussie! Aussie!
Oi! Oi! Oi!
What are you up to here my boy?

not allowed to mine like this in your own land
so you're here to turn a profit
on Khoisan fynbos-sand

you say you have good policies firmly in place
to repair this environmental disgrace
but let's just call it RAPE!

the truth is you definitely know
you can't rehabilitate
what took ten thousand years or so

who gave you the permission
to defile these burial sites?
what ethical perversion gave you these rights?

and yes you've promised to mitigate and restore
but once a virgin's been defiled
she's not a virgin anymore

these pristine systems have been around too long

for you to abuse our coast
and build your billabongs

this land abounds in nature's gifts
and beauty rich and rare
so to be fair

remove your tractor-scrapers
and your hard-hat mining crew
and go back to the land of the didgeridoo!

silver ball

she is the pinball wizard
from Brixton down to Walthamstow
she must have played them all
on this cold night she has no place to go

young woman from the estates
drab winter coat and worn closed shoes
black beret angled on her tar-black hair
her eyes half-lidded with fatigue

she holds a suitcase and a red-striped moving bag

her life possessions are enclosed within
the train rocks on
another station and the doors slam open – then slam
closed again

a man alongside offers up his seat
an older woman flopping down
who asks in valley lilt "you tired my dear?"
"I am" she says deadpan "I am"

Green Park... the packed train screeches in
the woman goes unnoticed as commuters to and fro
she finds her safe place in the gentle rock of train
like mother's rocking hand upon an infant's rocking
pram

for single fare she rides the line
from Brixton down to Black Horse Road and back
she rides the track – again – again
that's how she keeps the black dog in

Oxford Circus clatters into view
I exit out and glimpse her through the closed window
as she continues on her endless loop
and I strong-stride away

the flipper doors snap back

her silver ball flies down the shooter track
her jackpot score is on display
the backlit sign declares... replay... replay... replay

mother of three

on a sunny winter's day
Bongeka Buso strolls down Blythe Street
from Khanya Community Radio
where she borrowed R100 from a friend

she ambles down the hill past the Good Shepherd
Christian School
past the turnoff to the golf course at Butterworth
Country Club
past Pick & Build Hardware and Techno Auto with its
blistered bargeboards
past SPAR on the left and PMD Outfitting on the right

an SAB truck with Castle Lager advertising rumbles by
as she saunters down to the busy part of town – to
Umtata Street
bustling with vendors selling oranges and multicoloured
cloth

then on past the crowd queuing to collect child grants at
the Post Office

at Shoprite she stops to buy rat poison for R29.99 for the
two little ones' porridge
a R19.99 knife set for Anathi her 14-year-old daughter
and for herself... a R24.99 Alnet ski rope –
"Suitable for all activities that require a sturdy rope" the
label reads

overwhelmed with sadness, Bongeka heads down to the
taxis at Lewis Stores
the change is just enough for the ride back to Tholeni
Village
to her hungry children in her small rondavel
where the debt collector will find the bodies the
following morning

crabs of Wexford Bridge

I take my seat at the slatted bar
kick my feet onto the well-worn rail
survey the dozen whiskeys on display
a pint-sized local next to me

travelling incognito I've come by the way
of the narrow road from Carrickbyrne Hill
that skirts around the elevated ground
stone-walled pastures far below

the lane winding towards the Irish Sea
past slate-roofed houses under leaden skies
past hawthorn hedgerows and dapple-trunk trees
past a man walking his dog

I'm not in the mood for small talk
but your Irishman engages me
unpeeling my origins and the reason for my visit
"Jaqueline O'Donnell in Dublin" I declare

"so you're an Orangeman!" he concludes
as if we're in the Marching Season
reliving Bloody Sunday's pain again
I'm not in the mood for conversation

I buy him a drink
"I like you anyway" he condescends
outside the fog floats in – silent as a Viking fleet
dim lights illuminate the empty street

"have you heard of the Wexford Bridge" he asks
I tender "no"
"they jump from the bridge" he adds
confirming my worst fears

"they commit suicide"
his eyes expressionless
the information jars
the town seemed nice enough as I drove in

the story takes an even darker tone
– cold as the clammy mist that clings to the walls
and drips to the cobbled stone
– welcome as a rabid dog scratching at the door

he stares ahead emotionless and tells me more
"the dead accumulate beneath the riverbank you see"
I down my drink
to drown anxiety

the monologue continues in his monotone
"the bodies lodge beneath the bank

and there they stay
the crabs eat them away

eyes first and then the fleshy bits
until just skin and bone remain
dangling in the tidal flow
they use hand-nets to raise them up you know"

the barman says it's time to go
we drain our glasses and depart
stepping into the pasty night
he turns left and I turn right

my thoughts unspooling
as I pace away
then swivel back to do a doubletake
of the little man in the tweeded cap

but the shadows have swallowed him in
and all I can hear is the sigh of the sea
and the murmuring surge of the stream
and the click of the crabs at the estuary

cheers bru

I made my way along the Kogel Bay coast to Kleinmond
to see you one last time
I was not sure it would be the last time
but deep within my spirit I knew –
my old varsity friend Norris stricken with Pick's Disease
and ALS...
I'd had to google it

I passed beaches where we had surfed together –Pringle
Bay and Betty's Bay when we were young and free
when the sky had no limit
when days stretched together
laughing happy days
suddenly I was at your place
welcomed by your loving wife Susan
you were sleeping but after a while you stirred
a shadow of your former self
emaciated to the bone by relentless muscle decay
gaunt and speaking in deep groans
like a wounded lion trapped between a rock and a hard
place

I said "howzit bru"
slurring the words you blurted out "I'VE GOT ALS"
like an anxious child delivering an important message –

your brain frazzled by this evil thing

after a while we parted
I said "I'll see you soon"
but deep within I knew that there would be no soon

I grasped your shrivelled arm... "cheers bru"
I turned to go
snatching one last look over my shoulder at your sunken eyes
and for the first time
I thought I saw fear in your eyes that seemed to be shouting "DON'T GO!"

I swivelled briskly and walked away fighting back the tears
Susan greeted me at the door
I said "I don't think I'll see Norris again
her eyes welled up as if she knew something I did not know
"the hospice people are coming around this afternoon"
she said
she smiled
we parted

three days later your daughter called
you had slipped into a morphine-induced coma

another three and your spirit had left
to play forever with the wind
and the waves
and God

chestnut tree

I'm back in London at the Princess Diana Memorial
Fountain in Hyde Park
at the chestnut tree where I laid the flowers
on the day of your Cape Town funeral all those years
ago
when I annexed this tree as my memorial to you
my Afrikaner mother that loved this park with its
avenues of plane trees reaching skyward like leafy
cathedrals

I have returned once again on this late September day
with hardly anyone about

yet inexplicably under your tree is a young infant girl
resting peacefully in her pram - unattended
it's drizzling slightly and the hood is up
there she is - alone

no one seems to notice... no one seems to care

then suddenly a young couple appear hand in hand with
their young daughter
to reclaim their child from my mother
as it dawns on me
that once again a child has been entrusted to your
smiling care

now a mother and her young son arrive
to collect fat sweet chestnuts cradled in the soft grass
and once again your generosity flows

a squirrel darts up into your arms that he now calls his
home

a robin plucks a flaying worm from between your roots
and you have fed your favourite bird again

the wind stirs and your leaves dance
just as you danced and danced
when you were young

fallen

a wayward leaf came floating down to me
and landed gently on my heaving chest
as if it sought to find eternal rest
it came from high within a pin oak tree
the rising autumn breeze had rent it free
abscised it settled lightly on my vest
its final destiny at my behest
long gone the days of youthful greenery
replaced by interveinal tawny-brown
the visage showed the battle scars of life
the epidermis creased into a frown
and edges split as if by thrust of knife
I held it fleetingly then set it down
upon a fertile mulch of afterlife

tell me I lived

Robert Sobukwe
our holes are dug
our coffins neatly aligned
our faces – masks

Robert Sobukwe
speak for us
write in our books
gather the dust of our blood

Robert Sobukwe
speak to me
tell me I lived
tell me I mattered
tell me I count

Robert Sobukwe
sing to me
sing a deep song
sing a lullaby
sing a Methodist hymn

Robert Sobukwe
hold me
hold my warm hand growing cold

Robert Sobukwe
gather my soul

As president of the Pan African Congress, Robert Sobukwe called for a defiance campaign against the pass laws in apartheid South Africa which restricted the movement of black South Africans. At Sharpeville police station 69 protesters were shot dead on 21 March 1960.

666

the man painting the railings of the Groote Kerk has a
pleasant grin
"a contribution would be much appreciated
I could get into trouble for letting you in
guided tours only up to 2pm"

I step back hundreds of years out of the Adderley Street
din
into an empty space
a silent past
on the panelled walls the coats of arms of families –
remembrance of the dead
the white Dutch Cape

pews packed in printers-box squares
families segregated
status segregated
a dark place not only for the lack of light
the church that turned its face away
away from the Slave Lodge just across Bureau Street
the church where even pews were bought and sold
Christianity decreed the order of the day
no cape room here for Islam or Khoi faiths
dominee in his pulpit
back against the wall
turned away from the merchandise of slaves
families bought and sold
fathers bought and sold
husbands and wives sold separately
children of no value
heathen commodity
breathing stock recorded on slave ship registry

the painter calls
"time to go"
there is another church more modest in design
De Slaven Kerk to which I'm drawn
compelled by urges I cannot forgo
up narrow Church Street
stretching up Signal Hill

crossing St.Georges / Burg / Long / Loop / Bree /
Buitengracht

up into Bo-Kaap past Rose / Chiappini / Morris /
Church street that runs up into Dawes
to the kramat of Tuan Sayeed Alawie
first imam of the Cape
keeper of the Slave Lodge keys
preacher of Islam

but this is not the route I take today
just a short walk up Church
past street vendors
galleries
antique dealers
coffee shops
then right on Long
I find myself counting as I stretch my gait
5 6 7 8   323 324 325   664 665 666!

I step onto the threshold hewn of Robben Island slate
1799 in black on white
the door of Burmese teak shipped from Batavia
with manifest of nutmeg and the souls of men
can this number really be?
the devil is always in the detail you see

inside – the beauty of an open church
ceiling of sky-blue and not a single boxed-in pew
mission to the heathen slaves at the lodge just across
Bureau Street

                666 away

a bridge too far

most words are not written in stone
but these words are
etched indelibly on black granite
so that we may not forget
Sayed Mohamed
West Sumatran religious leader laid to rest here
brought in chains on the Polsbroek in 1667
by the Dutch East India Company
political prisoner banished from coral beaches
for the sake of nutmeg
brought here to hew timber for Constantia homesteads

I am alone in this lovingly tended garden
on a warm Cape autumn day
alone save for the keeper of the kramat

"may I go inside?
yes of course – just please remove your shoes"

I step into the sepulchre
with its white-washed tomb and persian carpeted floor

outside through double glass doors
a series of rectangular pools
step down the hill
brimful of reflected sky
dragonflies hover on weightless air
water falls in shimmering curtains

no bridges here for water to run under

For My Father, Now I Know... by Tendai Rinos Mwanaka

Tendai Rinos Mwanaka is a multidisciplinary artist, editor, publisher and producer with over 70 individual books and curated anthologies published in US, Northern Ireland, UK, Cameroon and Zimbabwe. He has 5 music albums, with a new album, *For Mberikwazvo: The Winter After* (2025) recently released. His music is playing in at least 18 radio stations in US, Canada, UK, France, Israel, Brazil and Australia. He has hundreds of paintings and drawings, thousands of photographs, some exhibited, some published and some sold. His pieces have appeared in over 500 journals in over 35 countries and his books and writing are translated into at least 11 languages. His music can be licensed here: https://www.songtradr.com/tendai.mwanaka. Find him here: https://m.facebook.com/tendai.mwanaka

If I had known

That being human is tough
Heartbreaking, unforgiving
If I had known enough about this
I would have chosen to be a doctor
I wouldn't have thought being an artist
You can create permanent, perfect artworks
That wouldn't grow old and bleed to death with pain
To death, seeing my father lying
Dying on bed 35, ward 4, Chitungwiza central hospital
Mucous, sweat, medicines, his hand's skin tight, gorged
By drip after drip of food, chemicals....
His noisy difficulty breathing aggravating syntax to sense
I would have chosen, that week, if I had to choose again
To be a doctor, for doctors are controllers of entropy
And entropy increases with time, stupidity and anger
And my penlessness art can't make my father alive again
Not even in that week of terrible jungle of emotions
The doctor's time-machines connecting my father
And us to a time beyond and now
To different horizons, ages...

And as a doctor I would have fixed my father
So that we could have another night of
Arguing, philosophizing, ideating
Him sitting on his old broken chair

On the main house's veranda and I
Sitting on the steps of the kitchen open veranda
Him trying to make sense of the world
His olding brains couldn't reconcile to
His tabula rasa light dimming, declining
I am 51, he is 82, and I, whilst I can understand
The world that I mis-inhabit by staying in the middle of
Which is an artform I learned as a poet, a writer, an artist...
To commute with stories feigned, foreign, fanged, fanned
I wish I could have chosen to be a doctor!

Fishing

Watching the water gently flowing in a pool whilst fishing was my kind of heaven when I was growing up. What a hell of memories, invading memories! I am at my favourite fishing spot, we called it padziva rekwaBabamukuru Vincent, just a few metres off padziva rekwaVhere that had hundreds of green harmless snakes, I didn't want to worry about the snakes, so I wouldn't do dziva rekwaVhere alone, even though it had more fish. Good thing with dziva rekwababamukuru Vincent is you would be perched up the slope, shielded from August's chilly winds, a safer distance from the snakes. The art was in how we would call parts of the rivers by names of homes adjacent to these parts, pools, crossings: Dziva RekwaMandofa, pamadhiramu, paShupi, PaNyahoda, pamahwematsvuku, paZambuko, pamagarden, pamaBennard, Dziva Regwena, Dziva rekwaMatimba, paTanganda, Pabirira... And the art in fishing is what stories would invade and rock you, your very insides as you watch the water's waves, sometimes a small wind breaking on top of the pool, the stagnant gold leaves whispering on top of the pool as they go wherever they didn't know about. Sometimes dreaming of your face inwards, inside you, the fish teasing your line, hook and sinker...until one ravenous Gwaya (Tilapia fish), Nyamufika (I have always wondered, are these the young ones of Muramba, (Catfish), so delicious, and the spotted Nyamuteedza, slippery leopard spotted fish, and the Mburi (silver Tiger fish), gulps your hook in thinking it was receiving manna from heaven. The short frantic spurts of energy, the strengths of the fish as it fights the hook, pulling the line away into the edges of the pool, and you bracing in excitedly, sticking your legs as you pull the fish out of water. We fished for food not for fun, and don't we all live for food and love? So the more we catch fish the more our inner faces created soothing stories and by and by we depleted Nyajezi of its stories. Now we can only fish sand, and sand, and sand...the barrenness of our stories

The Womb of Time

The night is opaque blackness
its black furs and grey paints.
blinds eyes
so that they don't see
The beauty of hot darkness

I move with a cat's impression,
indifferent, aloft
In the dark night's sexiness
of a silent night covering us
with kisses of darkness

The images gives you
exactly enough distance
like saying the lord's prayer,
instead of saying an individual prayer
in times of difficulty
is like Children born with wandering hearts
arching to see what they don't see

Mandirata

We reflect on a thinker of the past that lie in the mountain of Bingaguru
Standing for the marauding warrior chiefs of King Mutasa
For the scars and wounds of the battle of Mhanda
As they splashed the red waters of their bodies, facing King Makoni's warriors
And the insurrection within, brothers fighting each other
Reminding one of the waters King Mutasa had refused to splash into
As King Madziva dared him to fight him on top of the pond
Madziva, as the meaning of his name, are owners of what resides in the pool, quite sure the lion would never win
A fight with the water beings in the water
Knowing these animals' strength lied in the water
But on land, the lion can fell any giant, so King Makoni was pummeled
Back to his evenly flowing veldts of Rusape
And the insurrections deepened, brother killed brother, sister killed sister
As swords were tied in knots of revenge
In this terrible battle of Mhanda
And generations dispersed carrying with them

The nascent smells of the battle
PaMhanda's blood still roars into my ears, generations later
With stories written in spilled blood telling
Which land belongs to which people?
As villages, kraals, families crossed Odzi River traversing northwards,
In the waves that came to be known as Mandeya1 and Mandeya 2
Into Tsonzo, Sorobhoni, Nyatwe, Honde, Karombe, Nyatate, Nyamaropa...
These becoming our old and new traditions, shift and ceremony
As Chatindo and Mwanaka, generations later
Are two men, two brothers who stood against each other quelling
The sons of Mandirata, the lion that lies at Bingaguru.
And these are the only sons of Mandirata that my memory can still recall
And I will not stop looking beyond you, Mandirata
Was Chitsutsumwa, Mhango, Mutasa... your father?
Who were your other sons as they rejected each other?
Crack each other's bones, munch each other's flesh, and drink each other's blood
Burn each other's names and the paths they refused to choose
I will continue toiling through the past

Knowing the answer is there where a hero became a name
Carrying myself into child-eyed dreams
As all the shadows of my ancestral selves come to me unbetrayed
Mandirata the lion that lies in the biggest cave, Bingaguru,
Muguhwo, the lion that lies in Karombe, who named himself Mwanaka
Munhuwumwe, Peter, Wilfred, you are my shadow that walks the red clays of Saunyama.
The shadows that allows my light to shine
And Mberikwazvo, Jonah, lying a few mounded earths from Munhuwumwe, his father,
I am the father to Mberikwazvo's light.

Silent journey from the East: Villages, Towns and Cities...

In Mapfurira village; life in this place undefines itself
In the stillness that you will become
In the east a low fog swallows Mouzi mountain's top and high vales
And Nyanga Mountain that contains rocks bellowing bewitching songs, decorating the low valleys that lives in you
In the days that are as soft as doe skin.

You know you have to take another journey again to the west where you have nestled in for 30 years
You wake up early in the morning to catch the 3 Am Trip Trans Bus
With unreliable timetables; sometimes it's a 1 O'clock bus, sometimes 4 am, sometimes Zupco Bus beats it to Mariga station.
Sometimes both buses breakdown and don't make it, you have to hike for 300kms
In these early mornings, raw wind soughs through trees, Summer rains swirls in the air, rain water pummels the ground, pools in...
Sometimes you become of muddy earth, falling into these pools of muddy water.

Near the gardens, you need four eyes to avoid the muddy pools
The nascent wind on top of the pools, pelting everything...

In these early mornings in Nyanga at Mariga station
As you wait for the bus to Harare, are sometimes of clear moonlights,
The eclectic moon rising above the rhythms of the departing night
Few stars are old suns, cancered with spots
Owls hooting from black shadow trees asking the moon for metaphors for the light

And as the bus fights through the jagged terrain toward Nyanga town
You welcome the Nyanga of temperatures that swings low in midsummer
You will find the Nyanga that always listen to its inner mischievous child.
Vicious, chilly, cold, windy, rainy......
And later, Nyangombe River like Rusape River gorges through the rough mountain dales
Though going the different direction from Rusape River, it whispers away from Nyanga Town

The sun is a stranger that will arrive later, flirting through tree leaves
The morning sun will find you as you curve through Juliasdale's holiday homes, farms, tourist resorts...
Furious mountain winds rearranging your life, sometimes breaking in through the windows of the bus
On your way to the towns: Rusape, Macheke, Marondera, Melfort, Ruwa...
To Harare of high noise, all these sitting on flat land that sprawls to forever
These towns seem like a desperate attempt to gather against the emptiness
Are different from the borderline towns of Nyanga, Mutare, Chimanimani, Vumba, Chipinge...
Where everything; the mountains, rivers, gorges, trees... presses against you, inside the bus.

A breakfast of a small bottle of pepsi soda and biscuits finds you crossing Rusape River in its quiet groaning moments.
Rusape River that empties into Save river catchment, where the lions drink from, into Limpopo river
Whilst her twin Nyangombe silently groans into Kairezi, into the mighty Zambezi river
Zambezi and Limpopo are the two lines that demarcate the land between these two great rivers of the south

And every river and everything in this land finds its way into the yonder lands of Mozambique, into the Indian Ocean.

Headlands shops hide on the left side of the road, beyond the small knoll, Homes are dotted haphazardly to your left trying to suburbanize it,
And the right turn winds up a small valley on its way to Chiendambuya

There is a song on the bus radio you have heard twice now in different buses, same place, of the gospel songstress, mourning about her departed mother
As you crossed the railway line near Half Way house, like an omen...
You thought of your departed father, who decided to stop talking to you and never uttered a single word
After you heard him once when he called your sister, Judith, by the name of his own sister, Tete Moddy.
As he battled the dark encroaching fingers of death that had surrounded him.
His mind lost to you, all you could hear that week were his groans of pain.
He now rests, maybe like the singer's mum, in peace, in pursuit, in nothingness, you don't know...
The rim and ridges of grief cuts and scores your heart with what you gave, now lost...

As the bus weaves and power strokes down the valley,
heading into Macheke River

You like this part of the journey, it is a demarcation for
you, like that ever shifting line of the sea
One side is the land, the other side is the water: you have
called it the soul in another poem, *Sands of Time: This
is my house*
Once you cross Macheke River into the sweet soft
Macheke town, you know you are back in the home you
nestle in the west
And when you cross Macheke River going to the east,
you know you are in the home that nestles in you
This area is the gateway to the two souls you have, or
that have you...

The wooded short distance between Macheke and
Marondera disappears before you know it.
Marondera has a sweet syrupy feeling, a well-built town
with modern buildings, unlike Rusape that decays in the
east
Marondera is a farming city, in the middle of the rainy
Highveld, warm temperate temperatures, soft sun,
breezy air...
Bromley Stores tell of a story of a town that no one
wants to happen

It's still a shop, some few homes to the left, and empty farmlands, ungathered that way
Melfort's four ways tells you Harare is near enough, has grown
Like Goromonzi, Ruwa... from a small shop 30 years ago into towns
Dotted on that line in that silent journey from the east.
As the noise gathers heading into Sunway City, Mabvuku
Turn Off, Msasa, Rhodesville, you know the noisy beast
That home you nestle in is absorbing you back into its navel
Until another journey to the home that nestles in you
A home in the east that never stops calling you back after all these years.
And you know when it calls, you can only answer, and that it might be tomorrow!

Memory House: I am my father's Son

After the night encroaching had wrapped her fingers around him
And the departing sun on the brim of the western horizon swallowed him.
And after 5 months, until today, 14 February, on his birthday,
I feel like I have slept through a winter barren of memories
But now the poet in me tells me I am near the safety I had wandered away from
As I hear his soft baritone voice booming in my ears.
"Aahh mwanangu ndaisazviona kuti wakafanana neni kudaro zvese neizvi, netsoka, nokutsinda uchifema..."
He says he realizes I look like him, even my voice, my feet, how I softly groan whilst breathing...
Memories of him are now an old voice that I hold in my hands.
As they are as ever-present in me, as I am ever-present in them.
These memories cataloguing the schedule of seasons

When I was young, I was his number one alter ego
As I pushed the line of authority he wielded...
With slaps, sticks, *chitiropo*, and a furious commanding voice

And I defied it all with attitude, mischief, and defiance
And as I became old, I learned to commute with his voice in me
That pushed me to go for things I wanted, wished for
And years before the departing sun on the horizons took him
I would talk to him in his voice, in my own voice

As we decoded one another's fractured seams, forms, shadows like the river rocking the lands away
Moving our things in when everyone else was sleeping
We lived in homes that we were still building
These homes being only the dwellings that could contain our souls
Wondering ambitiously but still unable to find the body that will enclose us
And a shadow inside our bodies constantly talking to the shadow outside our bodies
And now I ask my body to forgive me for the inadequacy I had over it...

God is dead?

We are that student looking for, "the seer that says your
grandmothers are unhappy, give them a little apple"
We are that student looking for, "the shadows that
whispers you are the prophet, open your own church"
We are that student looking for "the book that says God
is dead. I think it has black covers"

Meal Times

All breaths and plates of food,
Cup of drinks are numbered,
Once you get to your last one,
You settle in the soil

As Meal times become
a riot of sick and difficulty,
His once round appetite
leeched out through his heart
is how death might sing

Our little meals are small deaths
calling out to blue pumping organs

And it takes years of eating
to see a death like this one,
death from the kitchen!

meal times can be the state of mischief
that comes to those who walk away
from death to allow ambition
to withstand the limits of grace!

Grief

Grown old with forgetting it
Grief is grief's harshest critic
Grief is the other side of grief
Hanging in midair, sneaking in
Like the dark scent of flesh
Like a bruised fleshly decaying fruit

Grief is the black cat trolling right past me
With a lunar stare into nothingness
It's impossible imitating the crow's fangled cry
The kroonging harsh shiver of ravens
Five birds with beaks lifted into the skies
As if perched in a cat's blossoming insides

There are no myth songs
Where the dodo bird is the king
To the cawing crows, intelligent ravens
Better ugly duckling had stayed ugly
And grew into something
As green and sheened as I am blue

Not just blue, but azure blue,
Cobalt blue, hurtling over the river
Like a bolt of lightning
Grief is seldom black,
Sometimes its yellow or green
Or blue butterflies fluffing in the wind

Grief is the risk
You ran with your first cry
To know that it hurts.

The Names We Borrowed

We do not know we should walk
The earth with answers
To the questions we did not have

The names we have borrowed
Are what we are called by,
Not the no names we were born with

Water borrows momentum from winds
To dance atop the skies
Like Aleck Macheso's razor wire dance

The park

~~It happened~~
Maybe it didn't happen
~~That which happens~~
Maybe that which doesn't happen
~~When it wants to happen~~
Maybe when it doesn't want to happen

Soul

Understanding it is
Standing under it
As it stands inside you

Death

Here lies him she had loved
With the little her heart
Knew how to let out
How to bestow upon
The huffs of this mound

Earth

All those years
Of yearning
All those years
Of wanting
To be of it

~~Green~~ Arcades

The greens, greening
In yonder valleys, green
Summers, of our youths
Homages of little souls
Blooming

The river flowing

The heat of the wind
Carries the sun in the wind
Cases of cares, caressing
Contours of our faces,
Canyons, cavities, caves...

Deepening skies

To dance to the wind
To sing songs of the wind
To listen, to unlisten
To that which has no sound
The poet in him is at home

Constructions

The short lines of sorrows
And jagged lines of grief
He could count on his skins
As it sarrows away

People

We walk, we talk
We eat, we chat
We dance, we chance
We starve, we stay
We have, we hold....

Love

And summer
Descended
Like lies
We tell ourselves
When no one
Is listening

The setting sun

Higher up the horizons
Blushing in the departing sun
~~Like~~ Butterflies swimming in
And out
Deleting their sighs

Instructions

All those years
All those seasons
All those days and nights
All ~~that~~ have made him
And ~~that~~ have unmade him
All ~~that~~ he never had

Hate

Hunger his only friend
Anger his only enemy
Humiliation his fire
Stimulation...
Simulation...
Savagery....
Accumulation....

~~Cars, buses, lorries,~~

He was here
Beside him
Some days he feels him
In the tips of his fingers,
Remembering

Blue hills of home

He is here
Patched upon
This mountain

In the villages

We are here
We are there
Here is there
There is not here

Chapbook by Lorna Zita

Introdução

Neste chapbook, Lorna Zita oferece ao leitor não apenas poemas, mas espelhos, janelas e abismos. Sua escrita é visceral, delicada e potente uma expressão poética que nasce do íntimo para tocar o universal, traz à tona dores, amores, lutas e memórias que ressoam no corpo de quem lê.

Lorna escreve como quem respira fundo diante da vida: com intensidade, vulnerabilidade e coragem. Sua poesia, marcada pela sensibilidade e pela consciência social, nos conduz por temas profundos como a identidade africana, o amor, a saudade, a natureza e o silêncio.

No poema *"Mãe África"*, somos acolhidos por uma reverência à origem, à terra-mãe, celebrada em sua grandeza. África é fonte, ventre e raiz, e a autora, com linguagem simbólica e afectiva, convoca a ancestralidade e a força do pertencimento.

Em *"Ser Mulher"*, Lorna revela uma das faces mais impactantes de sua escrita: a denúncia lírica. A mulher é apresentada como flor e fogo, resistência e cicatriz, força que insiste mesmo quando tudo tenta calá-la. O poema é um tributo às dores silenciadas, mas também ao poder de transformar e persistir.

A coletânea alterna entre o universo coletivo e o subjetivo. Textos como *"O fim da dor"*, *"Desabo por dentro"* e *"Não quero ser poeta"* falam de uma dor que é íntima, mas comum a muitos: a dor do sentir demais, da saudade, do não-pertencimento, do desejo de existir sem máscaras. Aqui, a autora escolhe a palavra crua, sem moldura, como um desabafo necessário.

O amor aparece em diversos tons ora suave, ora devastador. Em *"Amores"*, *"Volta logo"*, *"Que amanheça logo"* e *"Quando o silêncio chegar"*, o sentimento é vivido com entrega total, com a beleza e a fragilidade que marcam os encontros e desencontros da vida a dois. São poemas que falam da ausência, da espera e do rastro que o outro deixa mesmo quando parte.

Há também um encantamento com o mundo natural. Em *"Mãe natureza"* e *"O que dizer ao mar"*, o eu lírico encontra refúgio no ciclo da vida, na dança das folhas, no segredo das ondas. A natureza é aqui um espelho da própria alma com seus silêncios, suas tempestades e seus recomeços.

O medo e o silêncio são tratados com particular profundidade. Lorna Zita entende o silêncio como espaço fértil onde o mundo se revela com mais nitidez e o medo como um mestre duro, mas revelador. Em *"Medo"*, lemos: "Porque o medo também ensina, / Nos mostra onde a coragem mora." Uma lição que reverbera por todo o livro.

Este chapbook é um convite à escuta profunda. Lorna escreve com o coração exposto, mas sem abdicar da reflexão e da crítica. Ela não teme o desconforto, não foge da tristeza, mas também não desiste da esperança. Sua poesia pulsa, vive e emociona porque é feita de verdade. Ao final da leitura, não somos mais os mesmos. Somos tocados por palavras que ardem e curam, que abraçam e inquietam. Com sua escrita firme e sensível, Lorna Zita nos lembra que a poesia pode ser casa, resistência e farol mesmo (ou principalmente) nos dias mais escuros.

Mãe África

África, mãe de todos os filhos,
Teus seios guardam o ouro do sol,
Tuas mãos forjam a terra com raízes profundas,
E teus olhos reflectem o céu de esperanças sem fim.

Teu corpo é feito de montanhas e rios,
Onde os ancestrais dançam com a poeira do vento.
Cada passo em tua terra é um retorno ao começo,
Onde o coração bate forte, pulsando a vida em cada batida.

Mãe das línguas e das histórias,
Teu ventre gerou reis e poetas,
Guerreiras de uma alma forte,
E sonhos que atravessam oceanos em busca de liberdade.

Mãe que é sol e chuva,
Que é dor e alegria,
Mãe África, nossa origem, nossa essência,
Te celebramos com amor e coragem.

O fim da dor

A dor é um grito mudo,
que mora no peito,
sem pedir licença,
sem dar respeito.

É sombra que dança
quando apagam a luz,
e mesmo em silêncio,
carrega uma cruz.
Será que um dia
Ela terá fim?

Mãe natureza

Verde que embala o vento,
rio que canta no chão,
céu bordado de silêncio,
paz que bate funo no coração.

Folha que dança sozinha,
sol que beija as flores
na alma da natureza,
tudo começa assim.
Num grito silencioso.

Viver é agora

A vida é passo e caminho,
é tropeço e direcção,
é semente em solo incerto
brotando no coração.

É riso depois da lágrima,
é sol que rasga a dor,
é tempo feito de instantes
e sonhos feitos de cor.

Amores

Chegam com olhos que brilham,
palavras suaves no ar,
invadem sem pedir nada,
fazem o tempo parar.

Crescem no toque e no riso,
no medo de se entregar,
mas quando partem, deixam
um mundo para relembrar.

Quando o silêncio chegar

Quando a chuva bater no telhado
e o vento sussurrar no jardim,
numa equina qualquer da saudade,
vais lembrar de mim.

No cheiro do café da manhã,
na música que toca sem fim,
no rastro de um sonho esquecido
tenho a certeza que vais lembrar de mim.
E talvez seja tarde.

Desabo por dentro

Paixão é quando o mundo desacelera
só porque alguém sorriu.
É tropeçar nas próprias certezas
e achar bonito o tom do vazio.

É perder o rumo do dia,
desmarcar planos com o destino,
ficar baralhada com uma mensagem
e guardar o perfume no caminho.

Paixão é relâmpago calmo,
é fogo que dança e some,
é o começo de um incêndio
que nem se sabe o nome.

Ser Mulher

Ser mulher é carregar em si a força e a fragilidade,
É ser flor que desabrocha e se vê pisada,
É ser fogo e água e sentir no peito o peso da saudade.

É ter o corpo marcado pelas mãos do mundo,
Carregar cicatrizes que não se veem,
Mas que ardem nas noites sem fim,
Onde os sonhos parecem desaparecer.

Ser mulher é saber que a luta nunca tem fim,
É erguer-se todos os dias mesmo quando a alma chora,
É lutar por um espaço que te querem tirar,
Mas seguir sempre com a coragem do mar que não se cansa de bater na praia.

É ter no ventre a dor de um mundo desigual,
Onde o grito é abafado e a voz silenciada,
Mas mesmo assim não se cala o grito do ser,

Que insiste em ser livre que exige seu lugar.

A dor de ser mulher é a dor de mil silêncios,
Mas também é o poder de transformar,
De resistir, de ser e existir,
Mesmo quando o mundo tenta apagar sua luz.

Saudade

A saudade fica no peito, um vazio, um eco,
Um rastro de passos que se perdeu,
Na rua onde o tempo parou,
E a memória é o único caminho que restou.

O olhar se perde no horizonte,
Buscando o que não pode mais voltar,
Mas a presença permanece no ar,
Como um perfume suave, que se espalha no ar.

Cada canto guarda o suspiro,
Cada canto tem o seu nome,
E ainda se sente o calor do abraço,
Que a distância não apaga, só transforma.

Saudade é um fio invisível,

Que nos une ao passado,
E embora o corpo siga em frente,
A alma ainda volta, ainda sonha.

O que dizer ao mar

O mar sussurra segredos antigos,
E eu, perdido em suas ondas, me encontro,
Como se cada gota fosse uma memória,
Uma conexão entre o céu e o fundo do ser.

O horizonte é o elo entre duas almas,
Aquelas que se buscam sem saber,
E as ondas com seu vai e vem,
Carregam palavras que nunca se dizem,
Mas que se entendem no silêncio.

No mar tudo se dissolve e se refaz,
Cada onda é um toque que traz de volta,
Aquilo que a distância não pode apagar,
Conectando-me a tudo o que foi,
E a tudo o que ainda será.

O mar é um espelho de tudo o que sou,

E ao seu encontro, me dou,
Sabendo que, em cada profundidade,
A conexão é mais forte do que a própria eternidade.

Silêncio

Há um lugar onde as palavras não chegam,
Onde o som se curva diante da ausência,
Ali mora o silêncio
Não como vazio, mas como presença densa.

Ele caminha entre os pensamentos,
Senta-se ao lado da saudade,
E às vezes, diz mais do que mil vozes,
Com a leveza de quem tudo sabe.

No silêncio, o coração fala sem medo,
As lágrimas têm nome,
E a alma encontra um espelho,
Mesmo que ninguém responda, ela se reconhece.

É no silêncio que o mundo se revela,
Despido de ruídos e pressa,
E o tempo, finalmente,
Para só para ouvir.

Medo

Ele chega sem bater,
Escorrega pelas frestas da mente,
Senta-se ao lado do peito,
E sussurra tudo o que não queremos ouvir.

É sombra em quarto aceso,
É passo sem dono atrás da porta,
É silêncio que pesa nos ombros,
Mesmo quando o mundo grita lá fora.

O medo veste mil rostos,
Às vezes, é o futuro incerto,
Às vezes, é o passado que volta,
Ou apenas o agora que não sabemos viver.

Porque o medo também ensina,
Nos mostra onde a coragem mora.
E é quando o enfrentamos de frente,
Que descobrimos a nossa própria aurora.

Não quero ser poeta

Não quero ser poeta,
quero só dizer o que sinto
sem precisar rimar com dor
nem vestir a alma com metáforas.

Quero falar do que me rasga,
do nó que fica quando o mundo pesa,
sem ter de transformar lágrima em beleza,
sem pintar o que arde no fundo.

Não quero ser poeta,
quero só escrever como quem grita
quando ninguém ouve,
ou como quem sussurra
com medo de sentir demais.

Quero ser palavra crua,
sem moldura, sem palco,
porque às vezes o silêncio basta
e o papel entende mesmo sem poesia.

Já não sou o mesmo

Aí de mim, que sinto demais,
que carrego o mundo nos ombros
mesmo quando ninguém pediu,
mesmo quando o mundo vira as costas.

Aí de mim, que sonho alto
mas tropeço nas pedras do chão,
e finjo que não doeu,
porque chorar em voz alta assusta.

Aí de mim, que amo em silêncio,
que espero sem relógio,
que escrevo cartas e nunca envio,
com medo do retorno ou do vazio.

Aí de mim, que sou inteira
num mundo que prefere metades,
que insiste em podar o que cresce,
em calar o que arde.

Mas aí do mundo também,
que não vê o que carrego,
que não entende o que sou
chama de fraqueza o que é fogo.

Que amanheça logo

Que amanheça logo, por favor,
porque a noite pesa demais sem ti.
As horas arrastam lembranças
como correntes nos pés da alma.

Que venha a luz, que rompa o escuro,
porque nesta sombra, só existe teu nome
ecoando nos cantos do quarto
que antes era refúgio hoje, vazio.

Não quero mais esse silêncio que grita,
nem esse travesseiro cúmplice das lágrimas,
quero o sol, mesmo fraco, mesmo tímido,
só para fingir que estou bem, que passou.

Que amanheça logo,
para que eu me distraia da falta,
para que a rotina me salve por um instante
do que sinto quando me lembro de ti.

Mas sei que nem o sol apaga o que arde,
apenas adia.
E mesmo no dia mais claro,
tua ausência ainda escurece em mim.

Volta logo

Volta logo,
antes que meu riso se esqueça do som,
antes que meu peito se acostume ao vazio
e faça morada na solidão.

Volta,
que a saudade já não cabe em mim,
transborda nos olhos, nas mãos,
até no silêncio do meu sim.

Volta logo,
porque tudo perde o brilho sem teu olhar,
as horas se arrastam frias,
os dias já nem sabem passar.

Volta,
traz de volta tua voz, teu cheiro,
tua luz bonita no meu mundo,
tua calma no meu desespero.

Volta logo,
ou pelo menos diz que vem
que há esperança no caminho,
e que esse adeus não é para sempre

effigies of a madman by Beaton Galafa

Author's biography

Beaton Galafa is a Malawian writer of poetry, fiction and nonfiction. He also teaches French Language and Literature at the University of Malawi. In 2021, his first ever poetry book, *This Body is an Empty Vessel*, was published by Mwanaka Media and Publishing in Zimbabwe. His other literary works have appeared in *Florilège, Il Convivio, Journal Poétique de Luna Rossa, Caustic Frolic, Mistake House, Stuck in the Library, Fourth & Sycamore, The Blue Tiger Review, The*

Bombay Review, The Maynard, Birds Piled Loosely, Atlas and Alice, South 85 Journal, Love Like Salt Anthology, 300K Anthology, Transcending the Flame, Betrayal, The Seasons, Empowerment, The Elements, Best New African Poets Anthology, Better Than Starbucks, Literary Shanghai, Eunoia Review, Every Writer's Resource, Corpses of Unity/Cadavres de l'Unité, Journal of African Youth Literature, The Shallow Tales Review, and elsewhere.

procession

we could all be water
dancing to whims of gullies
on our way to seas and oceans.
to be reunited with ashes
of the children we burnt
& bones of migrants
who wandered far off
dreams of empty skies
in the nights of desert winters.
we could also be dead.
our snores, sounds of maggots
meandering back & forth
through the rot of our flesh
until they are crushed by weight
of the universe's sadness.

from nowhere

read this tonight
on behalf of all poems
strangled in infancy
with their bones crushed
under rubble, along with
minds of their creators
who
floating
now wander in space
waiting for time
to rediscover their emptiness
and light the world
with a stroke of fire
again.

rituals

i don't know how
i should tell you that
day & night were birthed
in space to let us transition
freely into silent moments
after the last metal finally

cuts deep in the ground
like a spear in skulls of royalty
or a heap of mangled bones
stacked in a hole in imaginary
jungles.

in awe

the young stand there
staring at their memory
fidgeting away into nothingness.
their knees have been gobbled
by loads of bones & skulls
trapped in storms their ancestors
brew on seas and in the dust
of cities lined with grey storeys
that smell death.

broken fingers

count all the broken
fingers i've lost in
this procession. every
single one of them is
a brother & a sister
who went into a mist refusing
to clear. i no longer weep,
reclining on a chair of bamboo & sack
father carved an empire through time.

April

we crack shells
and escape to hills
we will quit again
when these forests
catch fire from summers
or the sawmill ascends
our sacred rocks to build an alter
for the sun.

illusions

i sit on a broken chair
in the face of a fridge that roars
and hums out its fatigue to walls
tainted by all shades of colour.
i love peace, i say to myself –
my eyes fixed on a tiny leak
the landlord failed to spot
on his last day of inspection.
the birds give me that – my mind
wanders off into the garden where
there's chirping and hisses
beneath rocks – themselves a corridor
to a loud stream beyond our reach
which a man swam across last night
and broke into our yard without
moving even a single brick.

jogging

the only weight you carry
on your morning runs
is your head, pensive
on whether you should've
just joined crusaders
rolling down the mountain
with logs & rocks
to crush bodies
of the last surviving
town.

empty gourds

the echoes you hear
take me to a past
i don't remember living.
it could be the breath
of my brother, his skull
hitting boots of a policeman
to c-r-a-c-k & offer him
another empty gourd.

treading mountains

these hills host fears
of a river's broken jaws
spitting water that seeks company
at the foot of the mountain –
a woman with a pile of wood on her head,
a couple rolling up tinted windows
of a government car parked on the edge
of gullies, and a man escaping the burden
of sudden wealth protruding on his belly.

effigies

i think of you
as a rich effigy
no one wants to touch.
given a chance,
they would trade you
for a god who's been
in their black shoes,
his toes sandwiching
each other in a frying pan
where a madman
roasts enough sand

to last him a post-apocalypse.

places

i studied in hills
i worked in rivers
i slept under bridges.
of all places
i found beautiful
the tiny church
they built for my brother
with a black cross gathering rust
on a leaking roof of mud & dust.

a lover's melody

this voice is wind.
a night in summer
lost in dust of towns
pursuing modernity.
its whisper, a melody
of a harp knitted with
palm sounds in the silence
after a night of intimacy
between lovers that killed
their selves for envy to reign
under the scorching sun
of a non developing nation
still counting its lost messiahs.

2005

i saw my brother
rising in smoke
in cloud & darkness
that cut through a mist
i hid my eyes in.
i count all small victories
in this world of constant loss.
the last image i have of him
is a raised hand to my departing bus.

silent rocks

this stillness & screeching
from a distance, where else
could they have gone.
places of sanctity where
humankind rises above clouds
to wine & dine with rainmakers
of these arid lands & create
a world of clatters & effigies.
i love Sunday mornings & songs
of birds until the craftsman knocks
on my door with his sledgehammer
pretending to do what he couldn't
on any other morning.

dosing

how do you do it?
when it comes
i lower my face like a god
carved in stone
& let the lids fall
into place as i attempt
to decode the barking of a dog
last night.
it is the seism of a tyre
trapped in ponds on a city
road that throws me back
into chaos of this world.

apotheosis

if there was a way
of telling the sun
to land only where
i wanted it to,
these walls would've
lifted me to the skies
& caged me in clouds
to sit next to their devil

& build an empire
on promises of a return.
i would've sent them
a moon & stars
to clear dark stains
merry children left
on their coat.

Pentecost on the hills

when you were away
they turned off music
to listen to the river
babbling over
rocks. instead
the Pentecost
descended with
god's fallen angels
and scattered winds
to all sides of earth.
now they sit down
wondering
if gods really come
through a tonne of tongues
or a soft whisper

to one cursed man
cuddling a mound
beside his broken bed.

a season of harvest

that morning,
seeing strangers
come & go,
what did you choose
between harvest
& a string of letters
to America explaining
how gods made you
an abode for stories of
Harlem & Manhattan
in readiness for your return
when time was nigh?

water

i wish i were water
dancing to a gully's drum.
i would not have to worry
over the next route
or how to wash sands
away to the oceans.
each season of rains
i would fold arms &
wait for a winner between
god & mankind to issue
commands
of destruction & baptism
on any calm day of the week.

cryptic

this game of masks.
what if God meant
other things when
he rested his words
after six days of
blowing air into
everything?
because foregoing
church to write
a poem is more divine
than watching a man
scream to the ceiling
when beyond that
is just some piece
of metal falling off
a lost spaceship.

we could've come

we planned
to visit one day
we would, we could
but the paths we had
taken would not allow
could not allow. we
simply hadn't accepted
yet the fate of our sun
when we followed
the beauty of its setting.
gods, forgive. we
wanted to visit one day
we would, we could.

tears

they saw me
i saw them
they wanted
to understand me
my legs & i
pulling
each other
uphill.
sweat dropped
where their feet
stood
silently
observing
their water
was tears.

a word of departure

i cannot fear
what may never
come
but if it left
it may someday
arrive.
i cannot fear
what will certainly
come
but if it does
i may tremble
not out of fear
but because
the madman
who made this effigy
will one day want to
enjoy blooming
flowers of his spring
alone.

Chapbook by Mondo Kobi Arnold

Mondo Kobi Arnold est un poète, écrivain et scientifique congolais, né en 1992 à Kinshasa, capitale de la République Démocratique du Congo. Il est diplômé en Latin et Philosophie, aussi Licencié en Relations internationales. Amoureux de la science et de la littérature et auteur de plusieurs poèmes et œuvres scientifiques. Sa passion dans la poésie date depuis son enfance. Sa poésie est marquée par une emphase sur l'humanisme, le vouloir vivre ensemble avec un accent particulier sur l'amour, la justice et la solidarité.

Note de présentation des poèmes

Dans cette série des poèmes, l'auteur partage son expérience sur la vie sous ses différentes variantes, en évoquant la complexité et les contradictions qui caractérisent les sentiments humains dans les circonstances distinctes, avec une combinaison des styles variés des vers, personnels (vous, je, il, tu) poétiques et un alignement à caractère dualiste tantôt à gauche, tantôt centré permettent une disposition organisée qui s'affirment à travers ces poèmes, exhibent autant de visions nuancées, émouvantes et émotionnelles de la vie, de la femme, de l'amour, des vertus, de la séparation ou encore du scénario que constitue la vie en société. Ainsi, entre l'adoration de la femme aimée et la douleur de perdre la personne qu'on aime, entre la joie et l'amertume, entre l'espoir et le désespoir, entre l'unité et la division, les valeurs et antivaleurs, entre la justice et l'injustice etc., le poète capte avec justesse l'ambivalence de ses émois et les extrêmes dans lesquels se plongent ses états d'âme.

Dans cette rythmicité d'ébauche, il soulève également en poétique que la mauvaise interprétation de la vie conditionne un mode de vie particulier, surtout lors d'une épreuve ou situation difficile, où cette attitude s'exacerbe, et peut influencer soit positivement soit négativement notre avenir, et quel que soit le milieu de vie où on se retrouve.

Enfin, un accent particulier est mis sur l'importance de l'amour, la femme, la force, l'espoir, les vertus, l'unité et la justice étant pilier et fondement de toute vie harmonieuse, juste et épanouie en société.
Quoiqu'il en soit, la vie n'est pas un chemin qui va vers nulle part, mais elle un tout qui peut conduire vers toute destinée glorieuse.

Le poète,

Absurde absolu

Savez-vous ce qui est absurde absolu pour un humain ?
C'est de chanter le chant chanté par Chantal, sachant bien que sa chanson chante des chantages, cantique interdit par le chancelier chasseur sage des cantiques des menaces ;
C'est de danser les jolivettes dans un rythme dan brownesque, danse jugée dangereusement étrangère pour le danakil, dansant toujours au dancefloor ;

C'est de marcher au pas maladroit d'un malabar de Madagascar, marchant malhonnêtement au marché malgache, sachant bien qu'il est malgachophone ;

C'est de vivre une vie d'ovipare vilain non vigilant, ignorant sa nature de vivipare, et vivant comme étranger dans son propre corps et spectateur de sa vie ;

Mais ce qui est absolument le plus absurde pour un humain, c'est de se trouver vivant sans raison de vivre, car la vie n'est pas un chemin qui va vers rien.

Ce qui est la vie

La vie, chose complaisante en être, est ambiguë...
Elle est ce qu'elle est quand on veut qu'elle le soit.
Une fête où on s'amuse avec lui et elle,
Parce qu'un don reçu par un patron.
Une course fréquente accordant importance
A la vitesse de courir, car il y a un prix à conquérir.
Une attente du bonheur qui tarde encore à venir,
Alors qu'un chauffeur boxe et fait languir.
Une valeur ajoutée à tout ce qu'on a acquis
De l'existence, avec assurance et assiduité.
Une relation où l'amour et la haine font la loi
Entre créatures créées depuis création du monde.
Un but qu'on s'est fixé affectueusement à atteindre
Dans le parcours en ligne, pendant toute durée vécue.
Une priorité qu'on accorde à quelque chose de valeur,
Parce que nature oblige ouvertement.
Une épreuve où on est soumise, évaluée sans preuve valable
Indépendamment de notre bonne volonté.
Une responsabilité rare qu'on nous a confiée
A tout gérer comme gérant responsable à la gestion généralisée.
Une mission temporaire reçue d'un être suprême,
Mystérieusement comme missionnaires habiles à la mission.

Un temps passe dans un balèze espace terre,
Terriblement organisé par espace-temps d'existence.
Enfin une lumière brillante, éphémère du monde dominant,
Car la vie est un tout, et tout est dans la vie.

Ce qu'elle est

Un être conçu en humain étant
Femelle dotant d'un âge poussant
Confus à gamine pourtant
D'un caractère spéculant
Hier jeune fille, cependant
Femme maintenant.

Un être spécial, Créé du ciel
Sortit d'un temps partiel
D'une forme de Gratte-ciel
Et dépourvue de non essentiel
Avec un esprit immatériel
Pour conquérir l'immortel.

Un être de main créé
D'un art calqué
Avec un fond taillé
Contenant des drôles de beauté...

Telle est ma femme d'été.

A toi m'amour

Quoi de plus beau,
Que d'offrir une telle
Expression de romance
A toi mon premier amour !
A toi m'amour !
Comme tu es belle,
L'être au doux genre,
Tu es belle, mon doux ange.

Toi dont le cœur est balèze,
Tu supportes les maux
Que le géniteur
N'a point connu.
Lors de mon téléchargement,
Tu taris l'arme
De mes yeux,
Quand me fait pleurer
L'autre, toi tu compatis.
Comme tu es belle,
L'être au doux genre,
Tu es belle, mon doux ange.

Tu comprends les murmures
De mon cœur et l'incompréhensif
De mon enfance,
Que le compréhensif
Lui-même n'a point compris.
Voilà que tu m'apprends
En douceur et en tout supportant.
Comme tu es belle, mon doux genre
Tu es belle, mon doux ange.
A toi mon premier amour
A toi m'amour !

Ode à la féminité

Que tu es belle, mon semblable
Que tu es belle, ma compagne
Tu es l'éclat de la créature
La colline sublime de l'âme
Tes yeux sont des joyaux
Derrière ton voile lumineux.
Ils sont comme un troupeau
De chèvres, Tes cheveux.
Suspendues aux flancs
De la montagne de plaisir,
Tes lèvres sont comme un pouf

De douceur, et ta bouche
Est savoureuse.
Peau d'orange de la cellulite,
Ta poitrine est généreuse,
Car elle est une voie de père
Ta joue est comme une rampe
Du canapé, derrière ton enferme
Tu es toute gracieuse, ma conforme,
Et il n'y a point de défaut en toi
Il n'y a point de disgrâce en toi.
Que tu es belle, mon semblable
Que tu es belle, ma compagne

Doux soleil et belle lune

De la surface de la terre,
Naquit l'éclat de la lune.
C'est un visage exagéré,
C'est un corps modelé
Par un artiste aimé
De Saint pierre et
Rejeté de Saint Paul.
Il n'est pas un diktat social
Non plus un machiniste,
Mais c'est un art appréciable,
O doux soleil, O belle lune !

La tendance va au naturel
Loin des mannequins photoshopés,
Car sa beauté n'exprime que la vérité
Quand le regard des autres
S'en trouve Modifié et altéré
Vous êtes laide et claire, ma plume
Ton vrai me chante l'amour
Et ton faux me crie mépris,
O doux soleil, O belle lune !

Une jeune gazelle pubère réputée
Plus génère que sa vieille.
Poitrine, pilosité, finesse des traits

Et du corps, les fesses et le bassin large
Sont un confort à sa vise
Viens, tendre gazelle au visage glabre
Glanons les ingrédients de la jeunesse
Et nous écrirons notre faste,
O doux soleil, O belle lune !

Le sourire est enveloppant,
Avec des lèvres charnues et sensuelles,
Bien pulpées et appétissant.
Il dégage une expression de douceur,
Avec un regard lumineux et ouvert,
Et des sourcils en bonne posture
A la mode au rendez-vous
O doux soleil, O belle lune.
Telle est la lune, à la féminité.

Femme de distinction

Je suis témoin de la vie, le creux opuscule
Quand naquit l'illusion d'un être,
Dans le vide de l'inconnu et de l'oubli d'épisode,
Sa voix me ravivait le désir de naître
Et son amour me rassurait joie.

Je suis spectateur de l'amour, aux yeux de marque
D'une conscience tranquille,
Dans le froid et la peur de l'autre fébrile,
Ses intentions affables m'inspiraient confiance
Et son adresse m'était une bâtisse réussie.

Je suis compagnon de lutte, au temps d'orage,
Jouxte des cantiques impossibles de ma ville,
Des commérages et dénigrements de son semblable,
Qui parfois échouait sous ma clairvoyance
Et sa ténacité me sortait d'une expertise aguichante.

Je suis partisan de la foi, telle est ma voie,
Mon antre et mon agir me sont un mot maître
Ainsi mes actions ne demeurent sans espérance,
Je suis une âme d'espoir, oui un genre d'ouvrage.

Dilection

De loin je t'ai vu
De près je t'ai admiré
Du plus profond de mon cœur
Je t'ai désiré
Et toute mon âme je t'aime
D'un cœur de saint
Tu es reçu
Logé dans une atmosphère
De la douceur
Près de la chambre tendresse
Couronnée des désirs ardents
Et voulant rester toujours près de toi
Jusqu'à la fin du temps...

Monde à l'envers

Le monde à l'envers,
L'amour n'est pas sérieux.
Seul le sel du poisson salé
Garde sévèrement sa saveur
Suave dans la sauce,
Seulement l'air heureux
Sait agiter sagement le vent
Aux extrémités de la terre.

Quand la peur des pères
Perdurent dans la guerre,
Des guerriers combattent
Au cœur de la mer et crient
Au secours aux secouristes.

Monde à l'envers,
L'amour n'est pas sérieux.
Oui, le sérieux n'est pas l'amour,
Seule la sœur de Saint Pierre
Sait sonner la sonnette d'alarme
Au son d'alerte,
Même si les soldats somnolent
Dans la salle de sport, salle de scène
Rien ne se fait comme il se doit.

Sorcières aux chaussures jaunes,
Joggèrent tout au long du jardin
D'Eden, où Adam daigne
Rencontrer Eve,
Dévastée devant arbre défendu.

Le Monde à l'envers,
L'air n'est pas au rendez-vous.
Le bonheur des débonnaires
Dément l'air à l'heure où
Les aigles volent au rythme
Des joyeux mais sans sérieux,
Car l'amour n'est pas sérieux...

Le pli à elle

L'adresse qu'on l'a montrée
La montre qu'elle a regardée
Le rendez-vous qu'elle a pris
Le prix qu'elle a payé
Le temps qu'on l'a accordé
L'accord qu'elle a signé
L'endroit où elle est connue
L'homme qu'elle a dit « je t'aime »
Le temps de son bonheur

Le malheur de son erreur
L'hôpital où quelqu'un est opéré
Le mois où quelqu'un est né
Le jour où quelqu'un est oublié
La nouvelle connaissance qu'elle a faite
La négligence qu'elle a témoignée
La relation qu'elle a rompue.

Ombre opaque

J'ai fait un choix
Le choix m'a réfuté
J'ai refusé mensonge
Mensonge m'a haï
Comme dedans dédaigne ailleurs
Alors que j'ai pris la décision
Celle de vivre Paul
Loin du sépulcre passion
Et près du désespoir amour
Adieu romance !

L'ironie du sort

Je suis sans âme
Je suis sans cœur
Et le jour m'arracha copine
Quand le moi la désirai encore
Ô doux Dieu des cieux !
Toi qui m'apprendras aimer
Au beau milieu des hypocrites
Qui m'incitaient jaloux
Où est la place du vrai ?
Quand le sérieux crie faux !
Mort à la romance
Qui de fois confus
Dans le conte des fées
O, mort à la romance
Qui de fois confus
Dans le conte des fées.

Après la rupture

Alors comment oublier,
D'un coup quand le souvenir
Demeure longtemps un rocher
Et empêche d'avancer ?

Le chemin devient prolixe,
Montagneux et infranchissable.
L'air semble opaque et difficile
A respirer avec rime.

La voix de sans voix du coq
Condamné et atteint,
Rayant le chant du jour
Sous le brouhaha du noir
Loin de conclave soleil.

Qui réveillera l'aurore
Dans les jours à venir ?
L'ombre du passé pensant
Passer en action aussitôt.
Au rythme actif et passif,
L'avenir demeure incertain.

Les lendemains crient décevants
Tort au larron du bonheur

S'est dissipé avec espoir
Difficile d'avancer, difficile de s'en sortir
Et voilà pourquoi on reste statique.

Nostalgie

Nous étions amoureux
Elle et moi, étions amoureux
Tous deux amants joyeux
Comme deux adorables tourtereaux
Qui se fleurètent aux heureux
Oubliant les règles des aïeux.

Nous étions amoureux
Elle et moi, étions affectueux
Tous deux vivants les jumeaux
Comme au beau temps vieux
Où nos désirs se croisent aux rameaux
Ouvrant la porte aux crémeux.

Oui, nous étions amoureux
Elle et moi, étions fous amoureux
Jusqu'à ce que ma rose attrape toux...

Ma vie nouvelle

Je vivrai ma vie
Sans elle je vivrai ma vie
Même dans le miroir d'un autre
Oui, j'avoue le bonheur
Tendresse et caresse d'avant
Douceur du temps et harmonie
Du vent
Presse le temps d'avancer
Presse le vent d'emporter
Les souvenirs.

Passé parti, présent présente
Salut futur à point
Au revoir nous d'hier
Enterre-moi cette histoire
Vite, qu'on la fasse disparaitre
Laisse la place à l'avenir
Je me donne chance à réussir
Chaque jour ma vie nouvelle
Chance à la nouvelle lune
Je vivrai ma vie nouvelle
Oui, je vivrai ma vie nouvelle.

Ma vie nouvelle,
Elle est difficile à faire

Mais pas impossible à vivre
Elle vivra loin de moi,
Ma vie d'enfance
Je t'amène
Dans ma casse à souvenirs
Souviens-toi,
Du temps de la conquête
Copain de ma copine
Conquérant accompli.

La Ballade

Sur le chemin du silence
Avance avec joie
Et ne laisse personne
Distraire en chemin
Car bonheur n'est pas
Toujours endroit
Où on prévoit...

Sur le chemin du silence
Marche avec promptitude
Et ne permet personne
Perturber sentier
Car objectif ne sera pas

Atteint dans un chantier
Plutôt dans un château.

Sur le chemin du silence
Prend rigueur et vigueur,
Vise l'essentiel en bloc,
Comme l'aimant en fer
Car réussite est facteur
D'énergie, croyance et caractère
En objectivité engagée.

Sur le chemin du silence
Réside bonheur et paix
Va en harmonie avec nature
Reste objectif et va droit au but.

Espoir de l'oubli

Il en est de ceux que la vie
Ne fait pas cadeau,
Ceux qui luttent pour survivre,
Ceux qui se battent pour être.
Dans le royaume du bénévole,
Mon ombre ne prend pas tour
Dans le cercle des éloges,

Mon nom ne loge.
Mon Dieu tant aimant,
M'a fait homme et
Doté d'une force solide.

Je suis l'oubli palpable
Dans les ténèbres de la lumière,
Mon mot ne vaut rien
A côtés du mont lien.
Ma voix n'entonne au quotidien
Dans leur toit
A tout moment en moi
Rivalisent espoir et désespoir.
Mon Dieu tant aimant,
M'a fait homme et
Doté d'une force ferme.

Quand mon ego est fait
Le rebut de tous,
La balayure du monde,
Mon désir d'être se dilue,
Ainsi ma fierté s'offusque.
Mon désir fantastique
Se taille en décroissance
Mon Dieu tant aimant
M'a fait homme et doté
D'une endurance accrue.

Voilà ma tête haute,
Et ma nature pesante
Conditionnent mon être.
Ainsi va la vie,
Ainsi va ma réelle victoire.

Cantique africain

Dans le fond du noir,
Se réunit un culte du soir,
Suivant une culture amère,
Amenant les gens à la mer,
Avec l'envie d'essor,
Mais dans l'ironie du sort.

Au bout de chaque cirque,
Défile un perroquet,
Sous le brouhaha grotesque,
Tantôt au rythme philippique,
Avec augure et joyeux augure
Mais qui ne laissant peu d'espoir...

Dans le toit du black
Se nourrit l'envie du blanc
Plongeant aux méandres négriers

Datant à la traite des noirs
Sous le délice du gâteau
Ignorant le dégout des récits

Au bout de chaque envol
S'entonne un chant du vol
Au profit du château d'Evol
Aux apparences d'un convol
Soutenu d'odeur du sénevol
Aux égoïsmes d'antivol.

Quidam

Comme il se distingue de sa nature,
De ses valeurs de trame
Courtisant le faux à son comble,
Et de sa raison d'être ;

Comme il est vrai que ta plume
Te reflète l'image de la couronne,
Dans ta société qui m'intrigue,
Et qui jaillit la décrépitude ;

Comme il t'arrive, parfois le trouble,
Sans gêne et ni malaise,
A renverser le bien de l'ordre

Au détriment de l'égoïsme ;

Comme ton humeur labile t'existe
A tout prix la convoitise,
Même dans l'atmosphère de solidarité
Sans songer à la tranquillité

Toi semblable divin, source de tout mal
Qui gangrène ton bunker
Mais aussi le centripète point
A tous tes tourments...

Ma défense

Parce qu'il joint son ombre
Qui jadis brave l'ordre
A côtés de cette tour d'arbre
Où ma défense rimera à sa défaite
Et jouera le jeu de sa conquête
Jugeons sa prose malhonnête
Corrompu et ennemi de l'honnête
Alors oublions son joug boité
Concentrons-nous au jeu d'été
Méditons le cantique de la solidarité
Peut-être que ce jugement lui aurait été
Rendu en toute tranquillité
Et que reviendrait l'esprit d'équité
Voilà la justice papotée

This Traveller by Jabulani Mzinyathi

Introductory Note

This poet, like many others, is a traveller. By day the sun lights his way. By night the moon lights his way. To borrow from Boris Pasternak, a Russian poet of old, the traveller has an ' audacious eye.' This poet's journey takes him to conflicts in Zimbabwe, the SADC region, Africa and beyond.

The steel yokes are still around. The chicks are still in the steel talons of the birds of prey. There still is the inferno ominously engulfing humanity. Righteous Indignation is the result. Somewhere along the way hope will be found. It is not blind optimism but steely determination to get the freedom train back on track after its derailment by those on board the gravy train.

This poetry chap book addresses issues like the proxy war in the DRC where Africa's riches become Africa's curse, recolonisation or enslavement, environmental degradation by kleptomaniacs, corruption, counterfeit history, patriotism, politics of self-preservation, political conflict, poverty, civil service rotten state, hypocrisy and moral decadence among other issues.

Join this poet now on this journey into the past, present and the future.

Acknowledgement

My hearty thanks to Tendai Rinos Mwanaka for going back to literary times and suggesting that I engage in creating this chap book. Thanks to the Zimbolicious and BNAP stables of vibrant poets and writers in general. I still learn a lot from what they pen. Thanks to all who find time to read what I also write.

Livication

Dedication according to Rasta philosophy evokes images of death. So Rastas talk of *livication*. This work is *livicated to* present and future generations. It forms part of the literary estate bequeathed to my grandchildren born and yet to be born. Ayden Farai Chesa and Kaitlyn Akudzwe Chesa take the lead. One day soon they will have to read these poems.

The Traveler

Needing no passport
Needing no plane tickets
Not riding on ferries
Nor travelling on ships
The traveller on a journey
Travelling around the world

Landing in devastated Gaza
Where life has become cheap
War criminals bombing Gaza
Reducing those lives to rubble

There in the jungles of DRC
Where South African soldiers die
While Malema questions why
Landing on South African soil
There to witness weeping and wailing

Getting to the White House
There where Trump runs his show
There where USAID is withdrawn
Till non tax payers and beggars wail
While impoverishing their people

Getting back to puzzling Zimbabwe
Where there is no freedom after speech
Where the Chinese with impunity destroy
Coming like flies to a decaying turd
These all weather friends of the few with mega deals.

Stolen

I was then taken away
Away from Lake Kariva
Away from Mutirikwi

Brought to their great lakes
Taught of their lake Huron
Eerie, Michigan, Ontario, Superior

Taken away from the savannah grasslands
Brought to the Tundra region
And to the prairies of Canada

They made me sing 'Baa baa black sheep'
To justify their stinking greed
Grasped the rules of the game - monopoly
To entrench values of hoarding

Then the cow jumped over the moon
And the dish ran away with the spoon
And meaninglessness of it all
Sailing miles from harsh reality

Second Routing

They had to ward off
Ward off tropical diseases
Then they subjugated us
With the bible, bullet and gun
In language , dress, food, ... we aped them

In come their friends from the east
Invited for the so - called mega deals
Just a euphemism for enslavement
Our natural resources going for a song
The unemployed driven into slavery
Nothing to show but just a pittance

Operating under shrouds of secrecy
The owners of the wealth dehumanised
Sold by the elite that grabs the gains
Nagasaki and Hiroshima will be child's play
When the potency of the poisoning starts to set in.

The Investors

Not with shackles and chains
No longer crossing the oceans
Dead bodies not thrown to sharks
Right here on the African continent
Joseph still sold by his brothers
Yesterday it was the white or pink man
Today the slit eyed heartless yellow man
Call this indignation, xenophobia if you will
This righteous indignation against evil
All that is remaining are poisoned rivers
The cyanide and mercury poisoned streams flow
All we are left with are death laden wells
Our own kith and kin sell us into slavery
With their concubines in tow off they fly
Off to France, Malaysia , Dubai just for leisure
Off they fly to China, India and Singapore
Leaving us to die of curable, multiple diseases

We are being sold for them to be in those mansions
While in shacks we drown in seas of putrid poverty
All they do is flaunt shameless profligacy

Trinkets

Just for a few bloody trinkets
Many you sell into this slavery
Hear the wailing of our people
While you show off your wheels
Obtained from the broken backs
Of the bawling oppressed masses

With your smile like the morning rising sun
You receive that cursed blood money
They have you under closed circuit TV for later blackmailing
Your villainy was long put on record
Now you take the side of these creatures
No crumbs fall from their high tables.

Burial Ground

The myth of invincibility
Reduced to smithereens
The sycophants put to shame
For their talk of immortality
Born of woman, he departed
Leaving the empty shells at home
The multitudes without medical care

The sun then set in Singapore
That precedent was then set
The profligacy is put on display
Flying first class to seek treatment
Only to return as mortal cargo
That one shunned that acre for reasons
All that is wrapped in a vile veil of secrecy
The gullible are then bussed to the acre
Sending off the remains of another landlord
The propaganda machinery at full throttle
Spin doctors unleash tale upon warped tale of heroism
Tales of alleged consistency and persistence
Unwavering commitment to the sacred struggle
Of liberating the masses sinking in stinking pools of neglect
Another narrative will be spun again
History is indeed the tyrant's mistress

Scattered

Their bonds solid
Bones you break
You in the shacks
See their mansions

Riding on naked village bicycles
Mesmerising top of the range
The gleaming motor vehicles
Travelling first class by air

Chanting their slogans of death
While they amass wealth
The minority maintains its bonds
The majority shows calloused hands

Trapped in a false consciousness
Stone blind to the 'we' and ' them' reality
Like cattle heading into a dip tank
Queueing periodically to be duped.
Impervious to the obvious lessons

Listening

I long, long said it
The counterfeit story
Now you say it yourselves
Tell us what really happened
Stop lionising yourselves
To bolster your entitlement
To bolster your hyperinflated egos
Yesterday we learnt of the downing
The downing of a helicopter
At the hands of a lone female guerilla
Then came the vilification over power
Later the narrative took an ugly twist
What now do we tell the nation
Now we hear there was just nothing
Nothing but that English erudition
And that cowardly refusal to wield the gun
What now do we tell the children
Are you going to do what is right
Get off your high horse and eat humble pie
The masses are mired in abject poverty
Those that bore the brunt of that bitter brutal war
Later to be sidelined by the mercenaries
Bob Marley had long seen it on the horizon
Those that bore the brunt remain quiet
Fear grips their minds as they are force marched

To listen to stale, crusty and insipid promises
While with impunity the opportunists loot
With the spin doctors now in overdrive
The new narrative is under hammer and tongs
The hare brained schemes we now know
That personality cult is still around
Thought the lessons had been fully grasped
The same dog that bit us in the morning
That same dog bites us in the evening
What did we do to deserve such a sordid existence

Friends Or Fiends

Where I had sacred mountains
Today I have battered , barren plains
The rivers that once fast flowed
Giving life to abundant flora and fauna
Now deliver a slimy death to my doorstep
The mercury and cyanide contamination
What did I do to deserve this strangulation
So you call these putrid fiends your friends
The future is now destined for the morgue
The vile smash and grab right under our watch
British colonialism reduced to kindergarten stuff
Democracy in the workplace dealt a mortal blow
Those days of slavery alive and vicious still

The yellow slave master wields the whip now

The Patriots

They shamelessly blip and blunder
Knaves' myopic minds fully on display
Teaching us about undying love
That we should love our country
Love it just like how they do it
It was just about a wrong bag
For besmirching our angelic names
With imagined law suits we pounce
The lessons in patriotism galore
Fat Swiss bank accounts for patriots
Fortified mansions at home and abroad
For the inevitable torrents may come down
Flying first class for world class health care
Patriots sending children to varsities overseas
We all will drink from the wells of patriotism
Never again to cast aspersions on patriots

Self Preservation

The inevitable is happening
The old giving way to the new
Look there goes the setting sun
The sun will rise again in the east
Look who is fingered for meddling
To the north the routing took place
The middle finger was long shown
The meddling in the west bore no fruit
Voices of protest in the South West
The deep desire for self preservation
The chocking isolation is fast taking root
The sale by date has long come and gone

The End

Now you hog the limelight
Now a gladiator in the ring
Enjoy it for the end is nigh
Into the trash can of history

There is no pot of gold there
There at the end of the rainbow
Go where they now rest in peace
Those that claimed invincibility

When they are done with the sheath
They do not want a second look
That there is your looming demise
The rabid dog must be shot dead

You will rue the day of your birth
Go on enjoy your illgotten gains
Take your dirty secrets to your grave
You are now a liability to your handlers

Gladiators

There is the looming show down
From a distance we saw it coming

The daggers are now drawn
Soon the clangorous clash of iron

The gladiators in the ring
Expectant crowds on the terraces

As they size each other up
A pin drop could be thunderous

The ultimate price must be paid
It is a fight to the bitter end

The clash of iron draws a frenzy
Time has come for the coronation

Terrible Twins

They were armed
Poverty beside desperation
They were an explosion
That was also an implosion

The rumbling of turmoil
Running in all directions
Everywhere smoke billowing
Then came calm after the storm

The Influences

I write what I like
Am a student of Bantu Biko

I will speak of the wretched of

the earth

For I learnt lessons from Franz Fanon

Those lessons from Paulo Freire
Forever treasuring pedagogy of the oppressed

I will learn from Ernesto Che Guevara
An aspirant of international citizenship

I will walk in the shadow of Marcus Mosiah Garvey
Impugning all unjust and immoral laws with vehemence

Drawing from the lessons of Mqabuko Nyong'olo
Nkomo
I write this, the story of my life

I will get a lesson or two from African luminaries

Among them John Magufuli and Thomas Sankara

Done And Dusted

Nothing remains here
The york is long gone
The egg white is gone
Nothing but the egg shell
There just is no passion
Just going through the motions
Just for those peanuts
The mercenaries are here
It is just like prostitution
All bereft of emotional attachment
Just all the clock watching
All day long pretending to be busy
Threadbare jackets run offices
Office bearers absent in all respects
False kings and queens of the earth
The hyperinflated egos on display
Service delivery dealt a mortal blow
The maggots writhing in rottenness

Littered Road

The road is now littered
Bottles of cough syrup
Youths sit by the road side
Girls turn to nocturnal creatures
Parading their private wares
The hunt is on for the dollar

The road is now littered
With impunity laws broken
Law enforcers turn into robbers
Peddling the confiscated drugs
Immersed in human trafficking
Taking bribes without flinching

The road is now badly littered
When did we become drenched
No longer cherishing working
Queueing for those trinkets
Blind to those hidden costs
See the road is badly littered

The Same Crowd

It is still the same myopic mindedness
That yesterday asked for Barabbas' release
Today putting that villain in the spotlight
The new hero to those holding infamous degrees
Those conferred in morgues at night
That the ten year old was ravished by that brute
Has now been tucked away beneath that praise
Today the minotaur basks in the glory of sycophancy
Yet that young mind is still gripped by the trauma
The rapist gets a share of the acres of media space
While her trauma is left for a few to contend with
This is the era of warped old situational morality

The villain now transmogrified into a hero of sorts
Today the rivers of trinkets flow to his doorstep
Tomorrow the chewed bubble gum will have no taste
Today that gullibility earns him the limelight
Those knavish refrains are said *ad nauseam*
It would have been comical were it not tragic
That there is a dire need for exorcism is plain to see

Chapter Closed

That chapter will be closed
There will be that bawling
That incessant shaking of the heads
The sad songs and solemn prayers
The transformation will be complete
The body ,the remains are the terms
The villainy is there in the whispers
The lies are said with much vociferation
The maggots feed to their hearts' content
What remains is the time white bones
The memories become blurred with time
That chapter will have been closed

The *Chitutes*

Jack Mapanje, that Malawian poet
Detained without charge or trial
Yes, by that demonic despot in Malawi
Compared them to that mouse with kleptomania
Chitute , amassing what it does not need

We have the *chitutes* right here with us
By any means necessary amassing wealth
While the poor and needy drown in poverty

Their consciences long became liabilities

Their yellow friends leave us with nothing
Cattle, goats and sheep rot in pits
Cyanide, mercury pollutes our wells, springs, rivers
Environmental management agents just look aside
The castration of the nation long took place

What became of the real revolutionaries
Where did these mercenaries sprout from
What is the source of this barren cloud
That barren cloud that bears no rain
Where did this sense of entitlement come from

To My Buddy

Is it enough to just say thank you
You have kept me going strong
Over the years you stood by me
There have been many raging storms
You have come with lots of calm
There have been multiple bumpy rides
Bumpy rides along treacherous roads
You have remained my shock absorber
Archers' arrows have been aimed at me
They have shot at me without missing

You have been my unfailing shield
Many a blow thrown at me you deflected
When everything was crumbling around me
You provided me with a shoulder to lean on
When friends walked away as the cock crowed
Just like they are said to have done before
You stood there and declared profound love
' When my soul was hurting deep within'
You were there cooling my parched throat
You, the never drying oasis in the desert of life
The safety valve where life steam builds up

You have been with me from days gone by
The days of pen and paper, lap and desk top
You are with me now in this time of minutea
When my mind suffers from that paralysis
The paralysis affecting many of my fellow bards
You have come along with the benevolent muses
Together we still walk in that garden
That garden of sweet, profound inspiration

Of Blips and Blunders

Juju call your compatriot to order
His discordant voice is nauseating
The SADC hymn book is wide open
So too is the AU hymn book
Let us keep quiet about the EU one
For then a tongue lashing will follow

Juju ask your compatriot what he sings for
Could it be a lithium or platinum mine
Perhaps what diamonds remain in Chiadzwa
Or somewhere some virgin arable land
What is it that has stolen his sight
Spare the boer and shoot Mbaura

A brazier left overnight starved of oxygen
The generated carbon monoxide spells death
Our compatriots turned into crocodiles' food
Bludgeoned to death in xenophobic attacks
Necklaced over spaza shops and other menial jobs
Juju tell Fikile Mbaura Mbalula *sesifikile eGoli*

Is it myopic mindedness at play here
Yesterday saying our doctors work in restaurants
Today wining and dining with primeval beasts
Look to the north and the trekking down there

Tell Mbalula *sesifikile manje* by hook or crook
It is the grim necessity that is prodding us

Juju tell your compatriot to stick to his lane
That he may avert a looming and certain disaster
Who has paid the piper for this discordant tune
Tell this Mbalula , Mbaura or whatever to zip it up
The economic refugees yearn to be back home
Advise him to always put his brain in gear first

Gweru

Right on the plateau
Forlornly she now sits
Is this the city of progress
Now just another eyesore
The retrogression evident
Vendors line the streets
A cacophony of voices is heard.
Fierce competition for customers

Servant Leader

It is just another myth
Reality tucked beneath lies
Servant leadership another gimmick
The jostling is for the feeding trough

The rate payers wallow in squalor
Cholera delivering mortal blows
In their fast imported cars riding
Oblivious of the pock marked roads

It is the era of warped priorities
Trinkets delivery takes precedence
The rate payers submerged by poverty
Reeling under mounds of squalor

Big boys with their very big toys
Riding rough shod on the poor's backs
Workers show nothing but calloused hands
Licking lips in caustic admiration of thieves.

Chapbook by Maria Manuel G. A. de Menezes

Residente em Luanda

Introdução
A poesia de Maria Manuel G. A. de Menezes brota da terra quente de Luanda, do sal do mar que beija a costa angolana, e da escuta atenta da vida, em sua beleza e suas dores. Este chapbook é mais do que uma coletânea de poemas é um retrato íntimo e político de uma mulher que escreve com o corpo, com a memória e com a consciência de quem habita múltiplos tempos: o passado da colonização, o presente das desigualdades, e o futuro por construir.

Cada poema neste livro é uma janela. Em *"Coqueiro da Minha Praia"*, somos convidados a entrar num cenário de contemplação onde o corpo e a natureza se entrelaçam num momento de leveza e comunhão. O mar murmura, as tainhas brincam, e a narradora rebola na água morna com liberdade e poesia. Mas logo, esse idílio se quebra, e a realidade chama de volta à cidade metáfora do quotidiano que insiste em interromper o sonho.

A autora transita com maestria entre o encantamento e a denúncia. Em *"Mangal"*, por exemplo, a devastação ambiental é narrada com dor e saudade, como quem vê morrer um pedaço da infância. Já *"Zungueiras do Mussulo"* é um canto de exaltação à força feminina mulheres que caminham, trabalham, sustentam lares, com coragem e dignidade. Maria lhes oferece voz e visibilidade, revelando as cores e os ritmos da economia informal urbana com profunda empatia.

"Por África" e *"Não ao Racismo"* dialogam com um grito coletivo: São poemas-manifesto. Neles, a autora convoca à consciência histórica e social, à justiça, à fraternidade. Há uma África que clama, que sofre, mas também resiste. E a poeta não se cala: ela escreve como quem se recusa ao silêncio diante da injustiça.

A migração, tema global e contemporâneo, aparece com sensibilidade em *"Migrantes"*, onde o drama humano se desenha nos corpos que atravessam mares e desertos, em busca de dignidade. A poeta não olha de longe ela caminha junto. Há aqui um compromisso ético e poético com a vida dos outros, com os ausentes, com os esquecidos.

A autora também mergulha na introspecção, nos dilemas existenciais e psíquicos. Em *"O Que Fará a Minha Promessa?"* e *"Ausentes no Presente"*, há reflexões sobre promessas feitas à infância e sobre as ausências que habitam os corpos marcados pela dor. *"Monte Perto do*

Céu" e *"O Som do Silêncio"* trazem uma poética de contemplação, onde o tempo parece suspenso e a natureza, mesmo em sofrimento, ainda pulsa poesia.
Maria Menezes escreve com honestidade. Em *"Conformismo? Não"*, ela afirma sua inconformidade com a opressão, com a indiferença, com as estruturas que aprisionam. Ela não quer ser conformista. E nos convida, também, a não sermos.

A coletânea culmina em poemas como *"O Poder de Poder"*, *"Gota a Gota, Clique a Clique"* e *"Stress Zero"*, nos quais o ritmo se intensifica e as palavras assumem uma cadência quase profética. São convocações ao despertar, à acção, à transformação colectiva. Em um mundo em crise, Maria Menezes insiste no poder da palavra, no clique de consciência, na gota de esperança que se multiplica.

Este Chapbook é, enfim, um convite à escuta do mar, do outro, de si mesmo. Uma travessia entre paisagens físicas e emocionais, entre Angola e o mundo. Um livro que pulsa, inquieta e abraça.

Lê-se aqui a poeta, mas também a mulher, a cidadã, a testemunha do tempo. E nesse gesto de escrever, Maria Menezes constrói uma ponte entre o íntimo e o universal,

entre o poético e o político, entre a dor e a beleza com a
coragem de quem ainda acredita no amanhã.

COQUEIRO DA MINHA PRAIA

O velho coqueiro caiu debruçado,
raízes na areia em crina a fartar.
Em forma de cone na água mergulhado,
prancha para no sol me acariciar.

Um concerto de ondas o mar murmura...
E na areia desenhada a ilusão ondulo...
A maré calma vazante no tempo perdura,
folhas, sementes, conchas, eu adulo.
Água solarenga a amornar...
A convite dela imerjo e volteio,
corpo seminu a rebolar,
minha pele morena em meneio.
Tainhas ao pé de mim, tão perto!
Simulam beijinhos as inquietas bocas...
E voltam à faina de baile certo,
em cardume agitadas um tanto loucas!

Deleito-me demorada na praia de coqueiros,
embalada no vento da ramaria dos pinheiros.

O estrépito motor lá longe e a realidade,
lembram-me de voltar para a cidade!

MANGAL

No descanso de pausas merecidas,
chapéu sombreiro e óculos de sol...
Na pele de décadas vividas,
isco, lanço e puxo um anzol.

O tom azul e verde da água mansa do mangal,
é tão belo que temos num só o mar e o lago!
Faz chorar ver destruir beleza natural,
apenas me conforta a brisa num afago!

O escondido e tufado das copas no mangal!
A paliçada castanha de raízes esbeltas na vazante!
Fazem imaginar a efervescente vida animal,
desde lua nova à lua em quarto minguante.

Dois caranguejos assustadiços nos espiam...
Na areia onde corriam em esquadra e ilharga!
Onde o choco e a *mabanga* se escondiam,
hoje a areia é desnudada pela draga.

Memórias despertadas pelo mangal.
Saudade de ontem, saudade de ti.
Voltarei sempre, voltarei desigual...
Á destruição do mangal eu assisti!

ZUNGUEIRAS DO MUSSULO

Andam duas três e quatro, ar jocoso,
passo ligeiro pela areia do mar.
As cores balançam no gingar airoso,
tagarelas oferecem preço para cativar.

Agitam o rolo de roupa colorido:
Panos, túnicas, saias, calças,
Um arco-íris ao vento corrido
- Amiga, olha vestidos sem alças!

Com a conversa do preço falada,
uma peça pela vaidade ou pelo coração.
Delas foi na *zunga* a jornada,
cedo saíram para ganhar o pão!

Com firmeza e esperança na postura,
para revigorar, uma água na esteira.

Trouxas na cabeça pela faina que é dura,
É mulher corajosa esta mulher *zungueira*!
Menos pesadas e antes da visita da lua,
apressam os passos sacudindo cores.
Chegam cansadas do mar e da rua,
em casa aguardam-nas os seus amores.

POR ÁFRICA

Procuro nos montes, nos desertos, nos mares.
Procuro o quê? Não sei, apenas sei que procuro!
Talvez um grito que ecoe pelos ares,
um socorro com letras ainda no escuro.

Procuro nas casas, nas ruas, nos media.
O eco do grito de luta sem armas dos avós e dos pais,
o eco do grito de água fértil dos olhos da mãe
misericórdia,
o eco do grito dos sonhos de amores nas catedrais.
Um grito, um lápis eficaz para os filhos de Adão e Eva.
Procuro uma febre que sacuda a terra silenciosa de
África violentada,
um clamor que pare quem cria a treva,
uma visão de uma onda de força convulsiva que já tarda!

Procuro sem me cansar, até um gigantesco alarme soar em cada ser que pensa,
estrondoso rugir de montanhas enfurecidas de verdades,
um pesar de consciência dorido como cabeças presas à prensa,
procuro um grito fértil que germine em todos sensibilidades!

Dentro e fora de África, para África.
Onde procuro? Como se procura?
Em mim, em ti, um qualquer primeiro que exemplifica,
caminhos humanos e certos para a cura.

Não finjas cegueira!
Hei!
A catástrofe é tão visível á nossa beira...
Hei!

Homem Íntegro! Não queiras sonambular...
Não finjas que não vês,
inicia por ti um acordar!
Não vires a cara desta vez.

Corta pacto vaidoso, fútil,
recua nas barbáries em nome de Deus,
repugna saques e sangue de mina e fúsil,
foge de desonras pelos teus!

Olha a gente de olhar sonolento e enevoado,
sem o brilho alegre do verde-esperança.
A que lhes resta é porque te vê humanizado,
aguardam impotentes justa aliança.

Olha a pele baça! doente! suja! a mão não é mais
côncava a pedir...
Mal anda e de corpo rendido, tenta erguer a alma!
Na sua mente se mantém um sonho no porvir,
  "Que tu o vejas, e da vontade, tudo imana".

Ele vê-te, irmão.
Ah, o segredo é esse sim!
"Se tu também o vires, dar-lhe às a mão! "
Com constituição, com instituição, com o coração por
fim!

NÃO AO RACISMO

- Seu...
- Seu quê?
O primeiro cisco,
depois um golpe.
Na mente um belisco,
ecos e contragolpe.
- Seu...?
Tanta ignorância da humana lama,
cicatriz cerebral de ferida na alma.
Venham falas vivas em cada boca,
informe-se qualquer cabeça oca!
Um som de trovão *ionize* - ligue o mundo!
- "Os cabelos de enrolados fios, dos filhos na casa do rei Sol
são queratina dos átomos de enxofre, permissão do pai sol".
Um vírus falante - escolarize o mundo!
- "A pele escura dos trópicos ou das elevadas altitudes, é escura por pigmento não branco,
fazendo frente a raios ultravioletas causadores de cancro ".
Um nevão surja e lave infecta mente!
Pois há beleza, sabedoria e ciência, o ser diferente!
É preciso usar amor e racionalidade,
saber aceitar o que é diferente!

Não aceitar a vida com racismo,
lutar sim pelo humanismo.

MIGRANTES

No dia -a- dia dormem leve sono.
Leve porque a alma pesada mói,
no tempo longo de mau Outono,
a terra sofre e o corpo dói.
Nós dormimos bem, abençoado abono!
Mas alerta porque um irmão se destrói!

Atirados no mato, mar ou rio,
vão a pé, no bote ou falua.
Lançados vagueando no corredio,
da madrugada ao morrer a lua.
Com a esperança só por um fio,
fugindo dum país que já só tem rua.

Lá na terra não há labor nem lençol,
os homens se surpreendem a chorar.
A terra de impiedosas armas e sol,
obriga crianças inocentes a mirrar.
Há maus-tratos há miséria em rol,
sucumbem pessoas com dor sem par.

Vale a dúvida e sonhar com a sorte,
crentes na paz e noutra terra o destino.
Melhor que certeza na morte,
é enfrentar oportunista sem tino.
Vale procurar no Sul ou no Norte,
um cantinho de paz um alegre sino.

O QUE FARÁ A MINHA PROMESSA?

Prometi, na casa de cor verde onde corre pelo pátio a menina de pernas tortas.
Prometi, à criança ranhosa que sempre ouviu um não para as vontades,
e à sua irmã que conhece a ameaça pela comum traquinice.
Prometi, à adolescente que pensa que sonhar para ela não é permitido ainda que às horas mortas.
Prometi, aos meninos que dividem bondades,
para nenhum ter fome, nenhum chorar, nenhum sofrer doente em silêncio sem meiguice.
Prometi, à menina que não aprendeu as letras XYZ.
Prometi, aos jovens que tiveram oportunidade de começar um ofício,
que haverá uma mão amiga que ensinará o depois do ABC.

Prometi, às meninas mais velhas- mães emprestadas das mais pequeninas, e àquelas que nunca compraram um *batom* ou outro inocente vício.
Prometi...
Que superarão o trauma da guerra e da separação,
que destaparão o céu e vê-lo-ão estrelado,
e de dia, o azul límpido de águas nas suas mãos escorrerá.
Prometi ...
Porque a esperança é um amanhã no coração,
e porque acredito em mãos amigas num nó entrelaçado.
Mas...o que fará a minha promessa?

O PODER DE PODER

Macrocéfalos em braço de ferro.
- "A força é minha porque quero ".
- "Hoje ganho para amanhã ganhar".
- "Agora é a minha vez de conquistar "
- "O meu braço é longo, alcança o infinito!"
 Pasme- se, pois, atónito!
"Robotizados", insensíveis, deslumbrados!
Somar frações como ducados,
subtrair frações, dividir a união,
na terra mal-amada surge a confusão.
Vendem-se dilemas, oferecem-se leilões,

surgem súplicas e questões.

"Porque sou enteado no mundo"?
"Porque sou obrigado a escolher quase no fundo"?
... E os braços dos polvos, se cruzam nos jogos.
Nas ventosas a força do vácuo suga, e esmifra o globo, sem diálogos,
esquadrinhado a papel milimétrico.
Rasga-se brutalmente a pura seiva vegetal para o fio elétrico.
Esventram-se canais,
escadeiam-se minerais preciosos e metais reais,
enterra-se mais o punhal na terra ensanguentada!
Enlouquece a fauna sofrida, perdido está o Sul na terra marcada.
Sacodem-se as marés, baralham-se os cardumes!
Irrompe o espesso crude e azedumes!
Loucura de perdição, extravagante ambição,
na nossa terra iniciamos a destruição.
Dinheiro novo, dinheiro a mais....
Novo dinheiro, mais dinheiro e demais...
Envenenado com lavagem,
descontrolado e selvagem.

  Luxos e lixos bandalhos,
 reciclados, mas lixo no baralho,
 ... Chamam-lhes humanos!

Sustentam diabólicas guerras, insanos!
Só no dicionário existe fraternidade...
Criam ignóbeis rainhas de maldade:

O Genocídio e
O Fratricídio!

O SOM DO SILÊNCIO

O som do silêncio... Quem disse que não se escuta?
Quem disse ser pauta de linhas vazias sem eco?
Tem sussurros da paz da natureza,
tem diálogo com os teus sentimentos que segredam para ti.

CONFORMISMO? NÃO

Não sou conformista,
nem quero ser conformista ainda que o pareça.
Mesmo naqueles dias em que os lábios se colaram
silenciando-me
porque não me quero mostrar para não chocar.
Não sou conformista,
nem quero ser conformista ainda que o pareça.
Mesmo nos dias em que escolhi um falar discreto
porque estou feia nos meus pensamentos secretos de
feios que são.
Não sou conformista,
não quero ser conformista nem na minha condição
pequenina de aparência simples de ser ninguém.
Não sou conformista,
na verborreia desmedida quando uso meu bisturi
cortante no que digo meio irada.

Não sou conformista,
tenho o direito humano de não o ser,
tenho o dever humano de não o ser,
tenho maior condição, circunstância
e privilégio de não ser conformista.

AUSENTES NO PRESENTE

A mulher que eu vi a ameaçar,
de fulgor nos olhos capaz de matar,
em segundos a serenidade assumia
e a vontade assassina num ápice sumia!

Para de novo voltar um olhar de matar
e perguntas estranhas metralhar,
sem nexo, perdidas num fluxo completo
num olhar feroz centrado e inquieto.

Entre sinais e rios da loucura,
fugazes fios de lucidez e doçura,
quem sabe se oportunidade à demente
controle ausência de sã Mente.

À chuva outra jovem agarrada à demência
marcha, pára e ... continência!
Idas e vindas caminha na rua,
no solilóquio sem farda meio nua.

Não se disfarça a desgraça
da mulher bonita ainda com graça.
Que guerrilhas, que violências,
que tormentos nas suas vivências?
Ela sorri, talvez da loucura da gente,

que passa ao seu lado indiferente,
gente indiferente à mulher na rua
indo e vindo quase nua.

MONTE PERTO DO CÉU

Um Beija-Flor Malaquite
tão azul ... será que é verde?
perto do céu na montanha nevada
bebe água pura pela alvorada.
Uma girafa come com arte
frutos da árvore entre finos picos
molda os beiços moles em bicos
dançando um pescoço longo elástico.

Na floresta gelada elefantes,
e búfalos e javalis na erva;
no solo magma expelidos minerais,
do solo frio também dos servais.

Cervídeos às pintas de orelha bicuda
saltam manhosos na montanha,
assustam macacos de pelo e cabelos
que correm ao vento na floresta dos gelos.

Nas savanas capotas e chitas
- Campeãs de salto em comprimento -
zebras, rinocerontes e elefantes,
procuram água como antes.
Não sabem que o Monte sofre,
não sabem do glaciar que se perde
nem do voo dos abutres necrófagos
nem da gente secular no sopé dos lagos.

STRESS ZERO

Mil pensamentos, segundo zero,
a razão onde nunca quero.
Ideia uma segundo um
e o pensamento é dirigente.
Pensamento mil no tempo mil,
resultante inteligente.
Stress zero no coração
melhora qualquer ação.
Atenção: Foco e concentração!

GOTA A GOTA, CLIQUE A CLIQUE

Numa visão gigante, fria, branca,
branca de sal cáustico,
assustadora de inóspito vazio,
o incrédulo pode crescer.

Eu, madura, mais franca,
com melhor sentido "óptico",
desarmada no mundo... receio,
pensar nada mais me amortecer.

Mas espanto-me e calo-me na retranca
com susto e horror trágico.
Vezes há que estala um clique e me arredio
"Fica quieta, não mudas nada sem outro querer".

"Que queres tu mudar como alavanca?":
Ao ouvir um mercenário dizer cínico
que se tiver de matar mata de coração frio
e mais vezes matará por prazer.

Ao ouvir dizer o psicótico com panca
que é imperioso ir ao hospital (sádico!)
sentir o cheiro do sangue em assédio
 pois o sangue é a droga para o satisfazer

"Fica quieta, não mudas tipo alavanca"
Quando vês um criminoso desfilar sarcástico,
ou vês enlouquecer um visionário,
olhares impotente e nada poder fazer.

...Vezes há em que me estala um clique que diz:
"- Não fiques quieta, podes mudar algo como alavanca.
Ainda que não seja no hoje antagónico
ainda que seja uma gota do teu devaneio!"

Gota a gota, nasce a água para um rio correr.
Gota a gota mata a sede uma pomba branca.
Ainda que não seja no hoje irónico
ainda que seja só um clique, eu creio!

Clique a clique, creio podermos "crescer".
- "Não fiques quieta, podes mudar algo no mundo!"

Clique a clique uma vontade arranca
Clique a clique chega ao rico e ao político
Clique a clique desfaz-se um bloqueio
Clique a clique a mudança podemos ver

Se o conceito muda por poder e "estanca",
por sexo doente, ego frustrado ou antievangélico,
se aliciado pelo mafarrico vive - fraco e feio!

Então o conceito muda para o contrário - Basta querer!

Gota a gota,
a mente segreda-me...
clique a clique...
"Não fiques quieta, podes mudar algo no mundo!

CHLOOOC... CHLUC... PLOC

Chloooc... chluc!! chloooc ... chluc!!
... Falava o mar ao alvorecer
Meigo a desmaiar na areia.

Chloc-chloc-chloc... ploc!
Diziam em salva quebrados de ondas
Morrendo de súbito a mais pequena
Num cavado ao longo da areia...

Glossário:
Mussulo- É uma península na costa sul de Luanda. Com a maré cheia é considerada uma ilha.
Mabanga - Palavra em Quimbundo ou Kimbundu (língua Bantu de Angola), que significa concha de marisco bivalve.
Zunga- termo informal kimbundu que significa venda ambulante.
Zungueira- mulher vendedora informal, sobretudo ambulante.

Provoked Poems by Sebastian Jalameso

Poet • Satirist • Cultural Critic

Sebastian Jalameso is a contemporary poet whose work blends sharp social critique, religious reflection, and visceral imagery. His verse often interrogates power structures—political, ecclesiastical, and tribal—while remaining deeply attuned to language's material and sonic possibilities. With a style that moves between biting satire and meditative lyricism, Jalameso invites readers to confront complicity, injustice, and the frailty of human institutions.

Holier-Than-Thou

I once met a man—
A collar clasped his neck
Not like a leash,
Velvet-bound, white and stiff—
He was a Man of Cloth
God's own steward, he claimed,
Toiling in God's vineyard
Yet feeding not from the vine,
But from crumbs cast
By winged messengers
Across parchment pages
Of the Holy Book.

A learned man, they said—
He had read many books
In *one* Book.
He would quote, this man,
Being a man of knowledge-
From all the books
In *one* Book

He spoke in verses
As if Truth were his alone,
Each word dipped in gold
From Genesis to Revelation.

The crowd called him wise,
Wise in the way
That echoes in strained glass
And velvet pews.

The faithful flocked and re-flocked
His vineyard to knock at God's door
Knocking at Heaven's gate
Through his gilded pulpit.

Some rolled in the Spirit—
For a price.
Others pressed envelopes
Into consecrated hands
To unlock divine favour.

And he, God's man,
Beamed in the glory
Of a harvest he never sowed—
Reaping from trembling hands
And desperate prayers.

The Sentence

Thou shalt not rest.
Thou shalt not see
Heaven's deep foundation
Laid upon this Earth.
I—Lord of the Flies—
Have spoken.

Behold!
I shall remould thee, through moulting,
Clad in rufous feathers—
Thy new, cursed armour.
And none shall tear thee
From my grip.

Lo! I anointed thee now
With the graces of grime—
Pride that blinds,
Lechery that burns,
Envy, coiled and cruel.
Anger that smoulders,
Covetousness unquenched,
Gluttony wide-mawed,
And sloth that sings in shadow.

For thou are Fated,

So I declare:
To toil and sweat
To labour in vain,
In the service to none
But Me—
Lord of the Flies!

Primitive Civilisation

Who brought us this primitive civilisation?
Who moulded it to mould us?
From which primordial rock was it carved?
What river's mouth was the clay mined?
What potter breathed this spirit into it?

Who brought us this primitive civilisation?
What potter of delusions designed it?
What mind conceived this mimicry,
This hollow clone of culture—
This primitive civilisation?

Who brought us this primitive civilisation—
This idealised sculpted invasion,
This masterpiece,
Of primitive civilisation?

Who brought us this primitive civilisation—
Where women dangle testicles
From their earlobes,
And wear carcass hair
On their scalps,
And loin skins
On their faces?

Who brought us this primitive civilisation—
Where men—civilised and confined
In one-roomed houses,
Club their wives
While children are marking time, sleepless?
This primitive civilisation!

What sage imported this brilliance?
This primitive civilisation
Where moustachioed men
Play hide-and-seek
With moustachioed men
In blind-lit alleys
Behind closed doctrines?
This primitive civilisation!

This our primitive civilisation—
Where civilised women of polish and poise
Exude obnoxious slippery slime

Vomit the slimy secretion
In the mouths of their civilised men,
Locked like beasts
In heat.

And on stages, in digital shrines,
Dancers wriggle and wrench,
Twisting and turning,
Pushing and pulling
Pushing and pouting—
The crowd cheering, erogenous
In orgasmic rhythm.
Deflated,
The crowd eases
Satisfied.

Tell me—
Where did it come from,
This primitive civilisation?

The Liberated

In my country
Of liberated citizens—
Of pomp political rituals
Of enlightened liberators
March in patriotic footfalls
Crunching the earth
To mark our liberation—
They revel in the game.

They beat us,
for their game.
They arrest us,
for their circus.
And we—
we laugh through tears,
overwhelmed joy
and the sting
of their canisters
clouds of freedom's fragrance.

Like hunted beasts,
they smoke us
from our burrows,
in the land we call our own.
They summon our applause

for their gallant deeds—
their liberation of us
from the regime so cruel
they've worn its mask,
inherited its throne,
and mastered its seduction.

Now, we—
We are children
of conquerors,
raised on the milk
of betrayal,
nursed by flags
that never flew
for us.

Power Begets Power

Drunk, drunk, drunk
with inhibiting power that swells
like beer under the feet
of *ojur* insect
sitting in a pot in a cellar
watching its greatness rise
like dough.

It shakes its wings
in honour
of power that swells
to beget power.

Garden of Heroes

In the garden of heroes we had planted,
Thorns rose—unbidden,
Alien to our touch.
We waited for blossoms,
Not brambles and blood.

When bees came

To sip the nectar
And spin sweet combs
Of honey and oil,
Arrows flew—
Fired by the very heroes
Whose names crowned our hopes.

Still, we had waited.
Waited to taste
The honey of our labour,
To share in the golden yield.

But the garden now lies guarded—
By heroes turned wardens,
Dead-set
Against sharing
The oil of our sweat,
The sweetness
Of our collective bloom.

I Want to Hold My Political Wife

I want to hold my political wife
To cup her large buttocks in my palms,
As we rock to reggae and rhumba
Under the dim light
Of our dying republic.

I want to squeeze the bum-bum
Of my political queen,
Sway her hips in the breeze of a cool breeze
At Pearl of Africa Bar,
While I sip frozen beer
From the national refrigerators.

I want to touch the sacred *kwon-dud*[1]
That gyrating aphrodisiac,
Of my high-born bride.
Let my rivals gnash teeth in envy—
As I make love at the chambers of State Lodge,
And wet her with victory.

I must guard her oil-pot
From prowling *tunas* with hungry eyes.

---

[1] A Lango (the Nilotic tribe in northern Uganda) a term for buttocks. It humorously means the loaves of the backside. This is because they are soft and smooth like the rounded baked bread from millet flour shaped using the half gourd

My son shall plant a ritual gun at the entrance—
A warning to intruders:
Papa is inside,
Harvesting what he fought for.

My political wife is no mere lover—
She is a legacy.
Her oil is reward for my heroism,
For the bullets I paid for her bride price.
And you daydreaming fools—
Your withering stick cannot match my inheritance.

She is my immortal ride,
Wedded by Bishop Triangle Luweero,
Her breasts—ripe bananas in a season of drought—
Are mine to taste.
Her nipples sing when I roll my tongue.

Oh, yes—
My political wife is wet at the oil-pot.
She is sweet like Kakira sugar.
Profitable like Seeta Schools.
She flies me to orgasm
Like Uganda Airways reborn.
She quenches my fire
Like URA collecting taxes—
Faithfully.

For her Master.

Tribal Pheromones

I saw a bull sniff the air,
Sniffing for pheromones.
Gathering with his kind,
They jostled and shoved for a virgin heifer
The power of pheromones, compelling.

Then before my very own eyes I saw humanity,
Congregating in tribal colonies within juicy government halls.
The tribes with the strongest pheromones were there,
Marking every department with their potent scents.

Tribal pheromones, they've learned not to waste,
Depositing them only with strategic grace.
They know that better markings yield better chance,
While stimulants to intrusion intensify scent markings.

My country of scent markings is leaking,
The power of tribal pheromones is bleeding.
My land of tribal scents is sinking,
Everywhere the air is thick with their markings.

He without dominant tribal pheromones
Must fizzle miserably in the scent-marked zones.

My country suffocates in tribal pheromones,
Tribes with potent scents claim the juiciest areas:
To defend their mating.
To defend their breeding.
To defend their feeding.

Song of Village Chicken

A stranger entered into our yard
no ordinary caller.
My caretaker's grin—warm hospitality—
Beckoned me near;
his index finger pointed,
and I glimpsed the knife's gleam,
at the hour to appease the dog's appetite.

And –
the stranger's eyes devoured me,
a yawned nod of approved
for my age, my weight, my height—
his Adam's apple bobbing
in his long, hungry throat.

The two sturdy lads burst forward,
jaws serrated like sawteeth,
muscles coiled, faces set.

I raced—no finish line—
a lone pacesetter in empty lanes,
leaving heroism and hope behind.
They closed in as I squawked and darted
hither
thither,
wings spread wide,
heart pounding to the chase's drum.
beating to the rhythm of the chase
I fought
        I jumped
                I dove—
until their hands pinned me down.

O, breathless I cried,
a blade at my naked throat,
wings clipped, legs impotent.

Such is our fate:
to die without will,
without a grave.

The Cross for the Grave
(Dedicated to the late Mildred Atapara)

If God had been God
Who would have known the sorrows of death
And wishful meaning of life hereafter writ?
You sing hymns to lull away him
Ensconced in that seat of grandeur him
You twist-and-double-twist-lash
To wench yourself from the embers of hell
Knowing full-well God is not in hell
The flotsam and jetsam of God's image begotten
All those woes and predicament bent lame you
The omnipotent watching with the breath of death
And you're trimmed to think:
God must love us in death!

When you cross paths with life
And westward a setting sun journey
Mnemonic codes atop a dignified den
The flesh maggot-gobbled clear surrenders
Leaving model layout of Lilliputian stereotype
Severe and shining defiant against illusion.

That horrid look of the dented case for face;
That deep inanimate grin robbed of mirth;
That wicker-work a bulging statue defiant of fate;

That mockery of hope battered toll the knell;
That proud posture taught by the ethics of death –
Seen in summation guideth to the depth of death.

Why So Faint the Memory?

You died for me—yet why so faint the memory
Of prophets' whispers heralding your name?
You welcomed death you never earned to bear,
A fate foretold before the world began.
Still, why so faint the memory?
My days are veiled in urgent distractions—
Visions that dazzle, voices that enthral,
Emotions surging like untamed rivers,
Bright promises that glitter then dissolve.
Yet why so faint the memory?
Your words, eternal thunder in the courts
Of Pharisees and Scribes, unbending hearts;
Your signs spoke volumes—blind eyes opened wide,
Leprous flesh restored, the captive set free—
And yet, why so faint the memory?
I hear your voice in every gathering of the faithful,
Calling me onward to a new rebirth;
I hear your mother whisper, "Do as he says,"
And even Satan dares proclaim you God.
Still, why so faint the memory?

Your mercy flows to those who spite your name;
You kneel in prayer for friends and foes alike,
Entreating all to walk the narrow way,
To live in Truth, to bear the Light you give.
Yet why so faint the memory?
Had not the log obstructed my own gaze,
Had not wax sealed my ears to heaven's call,
Had not my passions waged their restless war,
Had not my stubborn will refused to bend—
Then I would surely, fully, remember you.

Parliamentary Infidelity

Into the August House strides the President,
Burdizzo in one hand, a sack in the other—
The carrot and stick of political theatre.

The chamber thrums with life, packed to the brim,
MPs huddled close, drawn by the President's allure.

With a grandiose flourish, he proclaims:
'I've come to make you political breeders.'
Skewed by the duality of his tactics,
They are forever entranced, aren't they?

With a fervour to purge, continues:
'You don't need the Opposition's testosterone,
Nor your own sense of otherness—
These do no build a nation.

I name you now the alliance of political concubines.'
Stereotypical of manga and anime,
They swoon for the President,
Clapping wildly, standing on toes,
Lost in the rapture of his charm.

Into the harem they cheerful march,
Relieved of their tottering wisdom,
To uphold the sanctity of governance,
And the hollow façade of democracy.

Dissolving in Spiritual Orgasms

Suddenly seized by spiritual orgasms,
They drown in convulsions,
Ruptured hymen of rationality.

Losing themselves in titillations
Of pulsating enthusiasm,

They wander into the realms of infirmity;
That animated sublimation now in vogue.
The induced spirit bawls,
Estranged from rationality,
Rearing to overwhelm,
Courted by the dramatis personae.
Now the spirit touches the erogenous zone of wildness,
Uncontrollable before the master of spiritual artistry,
Acting the illusion of omnipotence.

In a fit of petulance, the spirit reincarnates—
The spirit of art for art's sake ecstatically histrionic,
The spirit of the stage, by the stage, for the stage.

The master of spiritual artistry screams: FIRE!
The spirit collapses save for a few stitching movements.

Then the house bursts into a song of praise.

Tribute to the Womb

Rocked gently into sleep
By Mom's slow, soothing shuffling gait,
I awoke to hear Dad calling,
Mom's laughter dancing in the air.
How sweet it would be to meet them face to face.

I turned and heard their playful banter:
Dad: "Just a drop of the liquid now swelling like adipose."
Mom: "Spermic! No ... No . . . The nephesh breath!"
I joined in their shenanigans, kicking and bobbing,
The foetal and parental worlds linked in harmony.

In my early third trimester,
I could open my eyes, blink, and yawn.
Mom rubbed and massaged her belly,
Proud of me nestled within her.

She sang "Twinkle, Twinkle, Little Star"
And "You are My Sunshine,"
Cool, reassuring melodies I cherished,
Smooth and soothing, resonant songs,
Sung often when I arrived, wanting to cry.

Sometimes, Mom felt like a stranger,

Speaking in tongues not our own,
Filtered through a fluidic transmitter;
Who was this unfamiliar voice?
When I arrived, I protested her strangeness,
Crying until her smooth, soothing songs
Wrapped around me, comforting and familiar.

Mom loved hot sauce with chicken, garlic, and pepper,
Flavours infusing the amniotic fluid I swallowed,
Odorous molecules mingling with my own urine emptied.

After weeks in the sac, I arrived with a whiff,
A familiar scent reminiscent of what I gulped;
My mouth opening, sucking, tongue protruding—
Mom and I at the table at mealtimes.

Looking back at my first nursery school,
Flavoured with spices, garlic, and pepper,
Rich with social interactions with Mom and Dad,
Great teachers of inspiration and curiosity—
I must pay tribute to the womb.

From Libido to Creativity
Dawn breaks heralding a new day;
A juvenile sniffs the organ of generation, smiled skyward—
His phallic emblem peels, a burst of energy,
Bacchus, Aphrodite, Dionysus—orgiastic deities.

Laughter-loving, he pokes a virgin of his kin,
Unapologetic and craving, the squeaky wheel that gets the oil.
He danced on her back to a silent song,
Splashing in the Osun River, purified.

Another ritual, he squares her up emblematically,
Tongue flickering in fleeting romantic rhymes.
He danced around, blubbering,
His mojo scent tantalising, transfixing.

They romped through untamed vegetation,
Lusting, desiring, pursuing, escaping;
In the thicket, among the thorny shrubs, on the plain,
Serenading in heightened vocalisation—
Their spirits entwined in an inspiring sensual rendezvous.

From surrendering wholly to the deities,
They scale the rocky terrain of love, venturing,

Submitting mind, body, and soul,
Having imbibed from Ceridwen's cauldron.

This desire fuelled by primal energy,
This impulse transmutable to conquer rugged terrain;
Lofty aspirations and ambitions once only dreamt of.

A Wife on Sale

My wife is a clucking hen,
Herding chicks season without end.
My wife is a moral hawker,
Delivering carbonated tonics house to house.
My wife is a wild-medlar,
An *emaler* without luscious juice burst.
My wife is hybridized,
With Cladophora crown tendrils,
Flicked in fits of irrationality.
My wife has turned a red colobus,
In want of new habitat and ecology.
My wife is turning sixteen,
Her virgin breasts secularized.
My wife is a billboard,
For aphrodisiac supplements.
My wife is a display,
Her worth auctioned in glances,
Measured in the currency of longing,
Each smile a bid, each sigh a price.

She stands in the marketplace,
A figure draped in hope's fabric,
Her value etched in silent transactions,
Her essence bartered, her dreams for sale.

Three Wicked COVID

The media loves us unto death
It played and replayed this celebrated speech
Of our loving President
O, how I danced on the roof of my intellect!

"In these trying times, it's easy to feel down,
But let's not succumb to this pandemic's frown.
COVID-19 may have dealt a mighty blow,
But let's rise above and begin to grow.

Though our economy's taken a hit,
We'll rebuild together, bit by bit.
Let's not forget the lives we've lost,
But let their memory be a beacon, not a cost."

But now these other COVID variants;
The wicked three lurking in its trail:
COVID-Corruption, COVID-Tribalism, COVID-Nepotism.
Our scientists are gleaning for answers
From dead imported scientific rats.

Now I don't know of which I should die.

My loving President died of them three:
He died of COVID-Tribalism,
When the seat was sweet;
He died of COVID-Corruption
When the seat menaced him;
He died of COVID-Nepotism
When he bathed in his reflected glory.

Dying of diseases that kill important persons is my goal
I'm now considering dying of COVID-Corruption:
When the President died of COVID-Corruption
He received a twenty-four-gun salute;
COVID-Tribalism blessed him with a ten-gun salute;
COVID-Nepotism earned him a nine-gun salute.

A cabinet chair died of COVID-Sheets
Was honoured with a fifteen-gun salute
A doctor who died of COVID-Rats
Received a six-gun salute.

Last month we buried a businessman from Nakapiripirit
He died of malaria—
There were no gun salutes.
Last week we buried a teacher from Kwania
She died of childbirth—
There were no gun salutes.

I Was Born an Idiot

I was born into a stage of political charades,
A foundling with no choice in the script fate made;
I watched as my foster party's dark rituals played—
"Chew the cud," they urged, a wisdom masquerade.

My president hailed this act as high art,
His praises echoing deep within my heart;
Mentors feasted on secrets in every dark part,
And I, hungry to belong, let my conscience depart.

Now, a seasoned consumer of bureaucratic cud,
I wade through State House corridors slick and crude,
Forging deals with power, where alliances are skewed—
I sealed a comrade's fate, his freedom pawned and subdued.

They summon the media to weave a crafted lie,
Painting false convictions as the truth slowly dies;
In this labyrinth of deceit, our nation silently cries—
I was born an idiot, the offspring of corruption's sigh.

Cow on Heat and Tickler

With pomp, Omongo ascended into wifehood
Her in-laws drove the herd in their twenties
What a herd for such a fleshless girl for the tongue to eat with words!
The female tribunal, the aggrieved and sharp-tongued:
One had a mind not for silence,
And a mouth a cow on heat.

"Where can a man pass in such a fleshless body?" asked Cow on Heat.
"What a question from the lost virgin," answered Tickler.
"All bones rattling and crushing," quipped Cow on Heat.
"The nearer the bone, the sweeter the meat."
"If I were a man, I'd delete her from my list."
"But your list is already crowded with SDs."
"SDs with lazy chicken necks."
"And without, a cold bed and shrivelled guts."
"Soon I'll have no list."
"And soon you'll be shut like a scar."

"I'll hook him from that sickle cell."
"You for wifehood is a vagina dream."
"Men are not immortal to women of figure."
"Primly men can never stand the likes of you."

"Full-figured I am, ready for any man."
"Serious men look into and not at, women."
"For a quick pick, you're the best bet."
"No man has ever said no to me."
"Because you have never said NO to them."

They jostled inside to catch up on the hip
Tearing down each provoked thought;
Weighing wickedness against inviolability.

For not seeing the forest for the trees
Is wisdom borne of foolishness.

Song of Seventy-Seven

Let Mama sing for me—
A conjugal birthday hymn spun from sunrise and silk,
Her melody a single act of grace in a cacophonous nation.
Be silent as her notes fall softly, like dew on awakening petals.
For when I rise to this sweet song,
The nation stirs; it scatters seeds of rebirth
Across a field waiting for a new season.
Let Mama sing for me this conjugal birthday hymn,
A soothing balm that quiets the tired dirges

Of stalled schools and worn-out promises.
Her tune ignites me, sending me blazing like a shooting star
Across the expansive canvas of politics.
Let Mama sing for me this sacred melody,
Her solo, gentle cascade cradles my spirit.
I dance, wriggling in the pulse of her libidinous rhythm,
Spitting out joy in the purest act of fulfilment.
Let Mama sing for me this unique conjugal birthday hymn,
As I sway—back and forth—on the tides of renewed will.
For Mama's voice is the only incorruptible force in this land,
Where the clamour of the corrupt roars like a storm at sea.
This hymn is for me and me alone.
So to you, blind to the true essence of seventy-seven,
Hush now—
Only the Lord discerns the mystery of seventy-seven times seven.

Be quiet, and let Mama's song ring out—
A celestial anthem of renewal,
The conjugal restorative birthday hymn.

(Dedicated to the President on his 77th birthday)

Ode to the Breast

This human anatomy of eclectic meaning,
Embodying subversion, beauty, elegance, and desire—
May it be synthesized, may it be known.
In innocence it nurtures the young.
Inspiration flows from its rounded allure.
The mother figure, Venus, stands tall,
A symbol of grace, captivating all,
Isis feeding Horus, divine motherhood
The quintessence of care, a bond understood.
An important external femininity identity,
Its presence a constant grace,
Reminding us of life's warm embrace.
Nourishing the young, a gentle guide,
A source of pride, love amplified.
Yet now, in modern times, sexualized,
In this revolution of sensuality,
It has become impertinent, provocative, desirous,
Curves that captivate—a delicate lace.
Sensual, divine, igniting fire,
A spark entwined in longing desire.
But alas, lost to cancer and aging,
A devastating psychological toll,
An attempt toward reconstruction—defect,
A stranger in our midst, unsettling,
Unfamiliar, a silent twist.

Now sagging, weary in sleep's embrace,
Once firm, now yielding to time's cruel trace.
No rack can raise what age lets fall,
A foundation tottering, like a cobweb's call.
Preserved, a haven of rest,
A sanctuary where we are blessed.
Seven facets, a tapestry woven,
The breast—a marvel, forever unbroken.

Anus, the Political Maw

When Anus ascended to power,
We braced ourselves, hearts heavy with dread.
He came bearing an AS50 sniper rifle—
Terrified, we let him pass,
To seize what rightfully did not belong to him.

Yet his voice flowed divine, smooth as honeyed wine,
Words of a god, an angel sent to redeem,
His tongue wove promises of wealth and health,
A radiant future for the weary and downtrodden.
Vows seamless, phrases ablaze—
Like truth descended to mend the fractured nation.

But soon we glimpsed his true purpose: a throne of waste,

A seat for his ego, a siren for his gluttony.
And his hunger grew louder, a grumbling tempest,
A bottomless pit yearning to feast on plenty.
This ravenous maw, this greed, this insatiable void
Became a nest, birthing pseudo-anuses—
Each a shadow of him, his monstrous progeny.

They multiplied swiftly, spreading like dodder weeds,
Blending with us, their schemes cloaked in piety—
Each a shepherd with wolfish teeth concealed.
Some erected churches, sanctuaries of faith,
Filled with hollow prayers and stony silence;
Others built factories, teeming with condoms and wine
As if shielding us from the dangers they brewed.

Condoms littered the ground, wine flowed in streams,
And bold, libidinous anuses swirled in strange rites,
Libations poured to dark spirits,
Some crowned themselves as gods and goddesses,
Mimicking the pious, yet twisted in form.
Inspired by Father Anus, they forged their empires,
Spreading like tendrils of twisted vines.

Anus Mammon prowled the land, armoured in gold,
Resplendent, corrupt, seducing the masses,
His fingers thick with bribes, his smile a snare,
A web of opulence spun to dazzle and ensnare.

Anus Belial, lord of wine and debauchery,
Held sway in smoky taverns, crimson brothels,
His grin as wide as a gate, welcoming the lost.

Anus Moloch raised his grand pandemonium—
A palace of shadows, a den for his kin,
Where all the anuses and their converts gathered,
A court of gluttony, draped in arrogance and grime.

Anus Mulcibera crowned herself the goddess of change,
Chanting mantras of progress, wisdom, reform,
While feasting on the nation for her ravenous aims.

Thus they thrived, these insatiable gorgons,
Bending truth, sowing deceit, as if from the soil,
Till the earth itself wavered, corrupted,
Under the weight of their profane dominion.

Cracks in God's Weld

At a wedding feast, two souls were welded,
Beneath the arch of love, their fates aligned.
With vows exchanged, they became molten flesh,
The priest declared, "What God has joined together
No man can put asunder—"

The welding was a sacred art,
A bond forged deep within their hearts.
Yet as the days began to pass,
The seams of joy revealed their cracks.

In November's chill, another couple was welded,
Public smiles masked the quiet scorn,
Whispers grew in the sacred space,
As love's sweet glow began to wane.

"What God has joined together,
No man can put asunder—"
Yet cracks appeared in the golden frame,
Each flaw a flicker of love's fading flame.

He found her laughter, a jarring chime,
Her manicured nails, a talon's grip.
Her hair, once vibrant, now a tangled mess,
And her perfume lingered, a scent too strong.

"What God has joined together,
No one can put asunder—"
Yet beneath the surface, tensions swelled,
In the silence of love, their secrets dwelled.

She heard his snore, a thunderous roar,
His touch, once warm, now rough and unkind.
His hair, a wild, untamed spree,
And his lips, too full to kiss tenderly.

"What God has joined together,
No man can put asunder—"
Yet in the shadows, doubts took flight,
As love's once-bright spark dimmed into night.

With every crack, the weld gave in,
The hearts once joined now drifting apart.
Yet still they cling to that sacred vow,
"What God has joined together . . .," they ponder now.

APROPRIAÇÃO ERÓTICA DA ORALIDADE: CRÍTICA DO *EGO DO FOGO* NO ESPAÇO ANTROPOLÓGICO DO MATERIALISMO FILOSÓFICO.

Por Hélder Simbad
(Escritor e Crítico Literário)

Introdução

O presente artigo visa analisar a obra poética *Ego do Fogo,* da autoria do poeta angolano David Capelenguela, à luz do Materialismo Filosófico, que entende a literatura como uma "construção humana", passível de ser analisada racionalmente. O autor em questão, de modo global, analisando toda a sua produção, forja a sua poética a partir da oralidade africana e na obediência às normas estilísticas ocidentais e orientais. Com efeito, a nossa análise crítica incidirá sobre um dos três eixos propostos pelo Materialismo Filosófico: o eixo circular ou dos seres humanos; o eixo radial ou da natureza; o eixo angular ou da religião.

A Crítica Literária é um exercício essencialmente dialéctico, ou seja, de enfrentamento filosófico, pois, a obra literária constitui-se como desafio ao intérprete. A obra poética, por sua condição ontológica, é enigmática e os artífices da palavra costumam introduzir ideias que podem e devem ser analisadas sob várias perspectivas, fazendo da Crítica Literária um campo regido pelo princípio da multidisciplinaridade.

Após alguns anos de leitura das obras poéticas do autor que elegemos para o nosso estudo, compreendemos os seus meandros e, portanto, que tipo de atitude interpretativa podemos assumir face aos desafios que a sua poesia impõe. Partindo desse pressuposto objectivamos analisar a obra poética de David Capelenguela, intitulada *Ego do Fogo,* tendo como princípio teórico o Materialismo Filosófico, o qual concebe a literatura como uma "construção humana", pois trata-se de um autor cuja poética é moldada a partir da solidariedade entre a oralidade africana e a obediência das normas estilísticas ocidentais e orientais.

Breve Biografia do autor[2]

David Capelenguela nasceu na Huíla, em 1969. Vinculado ao jornalista desde 1990, no Namibe colaborou no Jornal de Angola e Angop, mas foi pelo jornalismo radiofónico que se notabilizou, tendo passado pelas rádios Namibe, Huíla, Cunene e Lunda Sul até 2020. É membro do sindicato dos Jornalistas Angolanos (SJA). Adstrito ao Ministério da Administração do Território, no FAS - Fundo de Apoio Social, de 1999 a 2014 foi técnico de desenvolvimento local da província do Namibe e, de 2014 a 2020, exerceu durante seis anos a função de Director Provincial da Lunda Sul. (Lunda-Sul)

Advogado de profissão, tem o grau de licenciado e mestre em Direito, pela Faculdade de Direito da Universidade Agostinho Neto, em Luanda. Mestrando (2018-2020) em Literatura de Língua Portuguesa pela Faculdade de Humanidades (Letras), frequenta actualmente o curso de Doutoramento em Ciências Sociais na Faculdade do mesmo nome da Universidade Agostinho Neto. Docente

---

[2] Informação conseguida por via de uma entrevista com o autor, em Fevereiro de 2022.

Universitário, exerce actualmente a função de Chefe de Departamento de Ensino e Investigação de Direito e Relações Internacionais da Universidade Óscar Ribas em Luanda.

Autor de 14 obras literárias, poeta, às vezes prosador e ensaísta, foi membro co-fundador da Brigada Jovem de Literatura de Angola, tendo entre 1993-1998 e 2006-2011 exercido as funções de Secretário Provincial do Namibe e Cunene. Membro e Secretário-Geral da União dos Escritores Angolanos, exerce também a função de pesquisador no Centro de Estudos de Educação e Desenvolvimento (CEED) da Diocese de Ondjiva/Cunene. Além das temáticas de desenvolvimento local e sustentável, tem-se ocupado na divulgação e investigação da literatura e da história da literatura angolana. Os seus domínios de interesse estendem-se à Teoria da Literatura e Crítica Literária, Linguística, Antropologia, Sociologia e Filosofia Africana.

Ego do Fogo no Espaço Antropológico do Materialismo Filosófico
De acordo com Maestro (2017, p.85), o Materialismo filosófico, como método de interpretação literária, é uma teoria literária que se basciasse nos princípios gerais de uma gnosiologia materialista, teoria do conhecimento organizado em torno da conjugação dos conceitos

matéria/forma, cujo campo de interpretação é um conjunto de saberes contidos nas obras literárias e com elas relacionadas organizadas sistematicamente como conceitos categoriais, e cujo objecto de interpretação são os materiais de literatura (autor, obra, leitor e intérprete). Jesus Maestro (2017:127), ao conceber o Materialismo Filosófico de Gustavo Bueno como teoria literária, compreende a "Literatura como uma construção humana que existe real, formal e materialmente e que pode e deve ser analisada de forma crítica mediante critérios racionais, conceitos científicos e ideias filosóficas".

Como *construção humana*, a literatura situa-se no âmbito da Antropologia; como *realidade material* efectivamente existente, pertence no domínio da Ontologia; como *obra de arte*, constitui uma construção na qual se objectivam valores estéticos; e como *discurso lógico*, em cuja materialidade se objectivam formalmente ideias e conceitos, é susceptível de uma Gnosiologia, isto é, de uma interpretação baseada em análises crítica das relações de conjugação entre a matéria e a forma que a constituem como tal Literatura.
(Maestro, 2017, p.127)

Todavia, para este trabalho, interessa-nos a definição de "Literatura" no espaço antropológico, lugar a partir do qual apresentaremos uma análise filosófico-materialista da obra *Ego do Fogo*.

Segundo Maestro (2017, p.130), o espaço antropológico "é o campo no qual se situam os materiais antropológicos", considerando a Literatura como parte essencial dos diversos materiais antropológicos que ajudam a explicar o homem no tempo e no espaço.
Essa importância que Maestro atribui à literatura pode ser compreendida por via do vasto repertório literário que hoje permite outorgar à Literatura Angolana o estatuto de uma macro instituição que reivindica toda a produção cultural produzida nesse espaço político-administrativo delimitado pela Conferência de Berlim, desde a arte neolítica às produções artísticas produzidas no período de ocupação colonial aos nossos dias.
O poemário *Ego do Fogo* de David Capelenguela só existe, embora se materialize tecnicamente, sobretudo no plano formal, como um produto estético que assimila as poéticas universalmente reconhecidas (simbolismo, surrealismo, concretismo, experimentalismo, etc.), porque resulta de uma cultura híbrida, multi-étnica, que deve ser inserida inequivocamente no espaço angolano.
A poesia de Capelenguela é a soma das suas experiências híbridas de sujeito cartesiano (forma e intenção estética) e simultaneamente africano (predominância cultural das tradições Herero, Nyaneka-Humbi e ovibundu), animista

em sua matriz cultural, de um racionalismo invulgar atravessado por eventos históricos sincréticos.

David Capelenguela integra o *terceiro período*[3] da literatura angolana produzida no período pós-independência (1992 a 2001). Embora tenha publicado o seu primeiro livro no final da década de 80 do século passado, é geralmente apresentando como um poeta da chamada geração de 90. Forjando quase todas as suas obras na oralidade africana, publicou os seguintes livros: *Planta da sede* (1989), *O enigma da Welwitschia* (1997), *Rugir do crivo* (1999), *Vozes ambíguas* (2004), *Acordanua* (2009), *Véu do vento: haikais e sonetos* (2011), *Gravuras d'outro sentido* (2012), *Tipo-Grafia lavrada* (2012), *Ego do fogo* (2013) e *Verso vegetal* (2014). *Ego do Fogo* é a compilação de 95 textos poéticos distribuídos em duas partes: a primeira parte é designada por *Primeira Viagem do Verbo* e compõe-se de 56 poemas; a segunda parte, *Segunda Viagem do Verbo* e compõe-se de 39 poemas.

---

[3] Em nosso livro, ainda no prelo, intitulado *Cortes Sincrónicos: Crítica da Literatura Angolana Contemporânea (1975-2015)*, reconhecemos cinco períodos distintos depois de Angola ter alcançado a independência: 1975-1979; 1980-1991: 1992-2001; 2002-2007; 2008-2015. É no terceiro período que colocamos David Capelenguela, mas é preciso alertar que, em termos de publicação, o poeta continua o seu trajecto. A razão do "corte sincrónico" é porque estamos em face de um mero procedimento didáctico.

A poesia do *Ego do Fogo,* enquanto acto criativo, resulta sobretudo daquilo que o estudioso angolano Jorge Macedo (1986) designou por poética de motivação oral[4]. David Capelenguela apropria-se dos materiais intactos que sobreviveram da colonização através da resiliência cultural dos povos Herero, Nyaneka-Humbi, Ovambo, e ovimbundu, modela-os com pinceladas da modernidade através da sua incorporação como instrumentos de adorno a realidades deslocadas, geralmente urbanas como se pode constatar no poema de abertura:

Despe-
se
e
despede-se
já (re) feita
acolhida do gemido

A brisa envolve-a
aos olhos hospeda o sol
 com o alívio e saturação

Traz nos pés
tecidos de hino

---

[4] Quando for mera tradução não estamos diante de apropriação como tal, na medida em que os poetas mais honestos como Ruy Duarte de Carvalho ou ainda Zetho Cunha Gonçalves deixam explícito a autoria atribuindo-a aos povos onde os textos se originaram.

o enobrecimento
beleza da Zebra

E a alegoria que faz
enfatiza a vaidade
de todo este herero

Canto Feminino
recanto *kuvale*
(p.11)
Ego do Fogo, em termos temáticos, circula em todos os lugares postulados pelo Materialismo Filosófico, que distingue três eixos no espaço antropológico:
1) O eixo circular ou dos seres humanos.
2) O eixo radial ou da natureza (o inanimado e inumano).
3) O eixo angular ou da religião (o inanimado e inumano, isto é, os animais como núcleo da experiência religiosa, etc.).

Depois de estudar a poesia de Capelenguela, conhecendo a sua natureza, acreditamos ter elementos suficientes para analisá-la em todos os eixos postulados pelo Materialismo Filosófico. Contudo, limitaremos a nossa análise ao primeiro eixo, o qual julgamos saturar explicita e implicitamente todo o conteúdo abordado por David Capelenguela.

Segundo Maestro (2017, p.132), do ponto de vista do eixo circular, a literatura adquire equivalência ante toda uma dimensão pragmática, histórica e política, a partir do momento em que os seres humanos constroem, cambiam, recebem e interpretam construções literárias, dotadas formalmente de conteúdos materiais (oralidade, manuscritos, livros, suportes digitais), psicológicos ou fenomenológicos (fábulas, histórias fictícias, personagens ideias, relatos míticos, explicações imaginárias...) e lógicos ou conceptuais (a literatura como forma de conhecimento e de expressão de ideias, reflexões e conceitos).

É neste eixo do espaço antropológico em que hegemonicamente localizamos a poesia de David Capelenguela presente em *Ego do Fogo* por seu ímpeto semântico.

A divisão da obra em partes não é explícita, parece arbitrária, porquanto assistimos a uma espécie de anarquia em termos de organização temática e acreditamos que teríamos possivelmente aqui um clássico da poesia erótica angolana, não fosse o número exacerbado de poemas e multiplicidade de opções temáticas, constituindo-se alguns desses poemas como meras redundâncias. Por consequência e por sugestão ao autor, suprimindo meia dúzia de textos que deixam transparecer alguma incoerência no meio de muitos bons textos, extrair-se-ia deste poemário pelo menos dois ou três bons livros poéticos.

Por conseguinte, em virtude dessa desorganização a que nos referimos acima, traçamos algumas linhas temáticas possíveis:

Naturalmente, **em primeiro lugar**, temos a temática que predomina a obra: os poemas eróticos.

A poesia erótica aqui reunida, embora se constitua toda como uma alegoria em virtude da apropriação que os diferentes sujeitos poéticos fazem da oralidade, deve ser encarada com outros olhos, pois, há, em alguns casos, narrativas escondidas por trás desse erotismo. Tal é o caso do poema "Zebra" (p.13) que alegoricamente satiriza a figura do anterior presidente da república José Eduardo dos Santos, vulgarmente conhecido como "Zé Du", destacando-se no referido poema a letra "Z", inicial de "Zé Du", que é a *Zebra, zagaia no trono do Zénite:*
zzzzzzzzzzzzzzzzzzzzzzzzzzzzzzzzzzzzzzzzzzzzzzzzzzz
zzzzzzzzzzzzzzzzzzzzzzzzzzzzzzzzzzzzzzzzzzzzzzzzzzz
zzzzzzzzzzzzzzzzzzzzzzzzzzzzzzzzzzzzzzzzzzzzzzzzzzz
Zebra, zagaia   no   trono   do   zénite
zzzzzzzzzzzzzzzzzzzzzzzzzzzzzzzzzzzzzzzzzzzzzzzzzzz
Zebra, zagaia   no   trono   do   zénite
zzzzzzzzzzzzzzzzzzzzzzzzzzzzzzzzzzzzzzzzzzzzzzzzzzz

zzzzzzzzz...... *no deserto com gaz(elas)à solta*
zzzzzzzzzzzzzzzzzzzzzzzzzzzzzzzzzzzzzzzzzzzzzzzzz
zzzzzzzzzzzzzzzzzzzzzzzzzzzzzzzzzzzzzzzzzzzzzzzzz
(...)
Zebra, zagaia no trono do zénite
zzzzzzzzzzzzzzzzzzzzzzzzzzzzzzzzzzzzzzzzzzzzzzzzz
zzzzzzzzzzzzzzzzzzzzzzzzzzzzzzzzzzzzzzzzzzzzzzzzz
zzzzzzzzzz...... *no deserto com gaz(elas)à solta*
zzzzzzzzzzzzzzzzzzzzzzzzzzzzzzzzzzzzzzzzzzzzzzzzz
zzzzzzzzzzzzzzzzzGRANDAZEBRAzzzzzzzzzzzzz

No quotidiano angolano *Zebra* geralmente remete para acções ou factos que não *deram certos*. Com efeito, a ideia de fracasso é reforçada pelo penúltimo verso (ZZZZZZZZ GRANDAZEBRAZZZZZZZZZ), de matriz popular, repleto de sarcasmo.

Zagaia, pelo menos na realidade cabindense, é um instrumento musical de construção artesanal, feito de alumínio, usado em cerimónias religiosas e fúnebres; emite um som que só se torna eufónico pela combinação harmoniosa com outros instrumentos.

Zénite reflecte o auge, mas, por inerência das outras expressões de conotações negativas, pela repetição do verso, assim como pelos versos subsequentes (no deserto com gaz(elas) à solta), trata-se de um "Zénite" de fracasso.

Escrever poesia erótica julgamos que todo o mundo consegue. Escrevê-la com arte e subtileza para transformar o indecoroso em material legível que pode circular livremente em salas de aulas, isto é, sair do comum, da vulgaridade, só com toque artístico, é bem mais difícil.

É muito raro alguém dar-se bem com o erotismo sem a prática sexual. Aliás, quando alguém consegue palmilhar pelos caminhos do erotismo, se não amou outra pessoa amou-se a si mesma como outra pessoa. A poesia erótica exige vivências, a activação de todos os sentidos, facto que nos faz acreditar que David Capelenguela é um indivíduo experimentado. A sua poesia é um misto de vivências rurais e urbanas, por vezes sem a definição de espaço, pois, em alguns poemas, os dois espaços colidem e o sujeito libidinoso perde-se em sua acção. Tal colisão resulta da combinação dos signos *rurais* com actos afectivos espacialmente indetermináveis. Nestas construções, o campo, o signo "oral" é adorno e sem delongas, essa atitude artística acompanha quase todos os poemas de David Capelenguela.

Alegoria (p.11),Zebra (p.13), Sedução (p.14), Meditação (p.16), Palma(d)nua(p.17), Fineza do passo(p.19), Observação (p.23), Unidade da forma(p. 28),Navegação das almas(p. 29),Esquematização do gesto(p.30),Memórias dos tambores(p. 33), Entre(fenda)aberta (p.36),Coito indigesto(p.39), Assobio de aviso(p. 55), Duodécima noção do fogo(p.60), A miragem que lhe ofereço II(p.62), A miragem que lhe ofereçoIII(p.63), A miragem que lhe ofereço V (p.66), A miragem que lhe ofereço VI(p.67), Sombra vencida (p.75),Porta do curral(p.76), Servidão da esteira(p.78),Perto da fonte(p.81), Acordanua(p.82), Som sedutivo(p.94), Apelo para o silêncio(p.97), 7 e 1 /4,Erecção(p.102), Servidão (p.105), Asas no dorso (p.107),Canção metafórica(p.108), Kotyitalukilo(p.109),etc., são amostras dessa **poesia erótica** à qual referimos acima.

Em segundo lugar, temos a **poesia de intervenção social**. David Capelenguela trabalhou e trabalha em instituições públicas, ocupando cargos de destaques. Conhecendo a configuração do fenómeno político em Angola, um dos assuntos mais complexos de que temos vindo a tratar prende-se com a relação antagónica entre a política e a literatura, escritor e política ou escritor e cargo público. Por via da poesia erótica, Capelenguela consegue disfarçar o lado interventivo da sua arte. Entretanto, parece-nos não querer inscrever-se no espaço da cobardia onde geralmente habitam os escritores que se autocensuram na esperança de conseguirem um cargo público de destaque ou mantê-lo. O poeta – como não se espera, pelo menos nós acabamos surpreendidos – ergue estridentemente a sua voz a favor do povo:

Roça-me o rosto de uma criança
com o brilho de salitre
o sol cede-me o mar

Encena-me a sociologia de Angola
sobre o questionamento do destino
que aponta-me para a penumbra
fome
corrupção
nudez
prostituição
embriaguez
males e modos de morrer antes de viver
Hino dos adivinhos (p.12)

O poema com o título *Agonia* mantém uma relação intertextual com o mito dos *Fulani*, que pode ser lido em forma de poesia na página 17 do livro *Ondula Savana Branca* de Ruy Duarte de Carvalho, com a diferença da menos-prosa[5] de David Capelenguela e adaptação. Em

---

[5] Expressão usada por Jorge Macedo em *Poéticas na Literatura Angolana* para se referir aos poetas angolanos que, depois dos poetas da Mensagem, primavam pela sintaxe rígida da poesia lírica

Capelenguela, o mito é a "democracia" que parecia ser a
cura para todas as formas de injustiças:
A pedra pariu o som
o som a sombra
a sombra o medo
o medo a fome
a fome a morte

Da morte
a corrupção da estrada
ficou cuidando de si
e seus irmãos
veio a **democracia**
que matou a morte
matou a corrupção
e matou a ganância

A ressurreição veio a seguir
trazendo consigo os pobres
que viveram
da morte da agonia

                                            Agonia(p.43)

A problemática dos antigos combatentes e mutilados de
guerra é aqui apresentando na sua forma mais cruel, não

---

em comparação aos poetas da geração de 50 cujos textos, no plano do fundo, apresentavam um discurso prosaico(narrativo).

muito diferente da realidade objectiva em que até indivíduos que, durante a guerra civil, integraram as formas armadas governamentais andam atirados ao abandono.
Passa um antigo combatente de
mu
le
tas
pára e pela vidraça
estende a mão
ao secretário-geral
pedem-nos esmolas

este diz:
não sei de que lado lutou!
e gargalhadas no salão
 até do ministro afim
Aniversário (p.57)

Quando Capelenguela se exercita na poesia contestatária, a voz rural dilui-se como se a injustiça não transitasse em contexto pós-colonial para essas sociedades mais antigas que também, administrativamente, fazem parte do território angolano. O simbolismo, o animismo e o antropossurrealismo, como diriam outros, dão lugar ao neo-realismo. Os signos *ruais* desaparecem quase que completamente. Podemos aqui criar duas teorias:

A primeira é a da evasão lírica – a poesia engajada pede mais conteúdo do que técnica. Poucos são os poetas que atingem a perfeição revolucionária de Pablo Neruda no espaço da literatura engajada. Não queremos com isso acusar de fragilidade a poesia de Capelenguela, mas a verdade é que grande parte dela, embora impressione, não atinge os níveis da poesia erótica.

A segunda teoria prende-se com o espaço rural como um lugar puro de acordo a concepção do poeta. Parece que, para o poeta, a ancestralidade e pureza africana se restringem ao *rural*, ao campo. Em virtude disso, os signos que daí derivam constituem o adorno da sua poesia mais elevada, daquela que nasce dos motivos mais sublimes, dos afectos, porquanto a poesia engajada resulta do desafecto em relação as políticas públicas que não impactam positivamente a vida dos cidadãos.
Hino dos adivinhos (p.12), Desolação (p.32), Agonia (p.43), Aniversário (p.57), Gemer intrépido (p.58), Democracia (p.69), Anestesia (p.70), constituem o corpus da poesia que resulta do desafecto, **a poesia de intervenção social.**

Em terceiro lugar, **temos a poesia que verdadeiramente reflecte as vivências rurais.**

O poema *Fertilidade* (p.18) é sobre o cruzamento entre etnias e pode configurar uma crítica à ideia de identidade voltada à pureza étnica. Imageticamente remete para um tronco geneológico em que ocorre o processo de miscigenação entre diferentes grupos étnicos.
Os antepassados abrem-nos o sol/
(..)
O fremir da terra
adverte a alegria da aldeia
que o canto **Kuvale** solta
ao som da acção do fogo

Resta-lhe o alcance
do **Kuroca** a dentro
e a formulação da estepe
que presta homenagem e o saciar
da conjugação

A pastorícia é uma prática muito comum entre os povos do sul de Angola. Enquanto os bois se alimentam, resta ao pastor algum tempo para rara reflexão. O poema "Gesto ruminar" (p.25) é sobre gestão do tempo. O sujeito poético é pastor e identifica-se no acto do boi. Da sua observação cronometra o processo de alimentação e digestão do boi que, depois de comer, fica arreado para o processo de digestão.
Estou selado no pasto

medito o sul
ao sol poente
Na superfície contemplativa
do gado
 confiro as horas
em **gesto ruminar do boi**
 e atinjo a exactidão da regra
é ainda primeiro dia
pela frente
conto cruzar-me com a chuva impiedosa
deste tempo

Mas pasto...
gravado no olhar gestual do gado
liberto as estações da lágrima descritiva
e finjo que canto o *djeyiei*
hino da circuncisão
ao ritmo ruminar do gado

Nos grupos étnicos Nyaneka Humbi, Herero e Ovambo, o gado simboliza riqueza, poder, estabilidade. O poema *Recheio* (p.26) desenvolve-se por via da prática cultural *Ukoi,* que ocorre geralmente quando um casal experimenta dificuldades financeira em sua casa, consubstanciada na perda e na redução do gado enquanto produto que permite regular a economia. Por vezes essa instabilidade deriva dos gastos vinculados a uma festa de

puberdade, pagamento de multa, cura de doença e do adultério. Casos há em que o casal concorda simular um assédio que geralmente se consuma em adultério pela predisposição masculina para o acto sexual extraconjugal. Em todo o caso, o presumível infractor deve pagar sempre uma multa:
Recheio
Na plataforma do vigor
A urgência da mudança
Governa a profecia do Ukoi

E o gado da sua multa
é recheio para o novo curral
a que se destina

Coro:
Vindes ver minha mulher
de mãos abanadas
venceu um curral
recheado de gado...

Amanhã será outro dia
Fertilidade (p.18),Gesto ruminar (p.25),Recheio (p.26),Vocativo (27), Canto idoso(31), Verbo da serpente(41), Recepção cerimonial(45),Tatuagem(52), Oku-luo(77), Lamento(80), Segredo do pasto (83), Dois tempos(84),, A chuva(90),Adágio do

verbo(91),Fecundidade (93),Canto Herero(95), Canto de apreço(98), Areias do rio(100), Transumância(106),etc., constituem o núcleo dos **poemas sobre as vivências rurais**. Em quarto lugar, **deparamo-nos com os poemas que objectificam a noite ou a apresentam como período de contemplação, criação e descanso:**

E poisa-me o gesto sintético
da oralidade poética
e passo a noite
imerso sobre os corais da tradição
sinais misteriosos
que alcanço sob a purificação
morte da noite

Morte da noite(p.34)

para mim nada mais interessa senão
o nada do agora
a morte é o repouso absoluto
da alma e do corpo

o diálogo fiel e directo
com Deus que nos chama
a vida é o intervalo
entre duas noites e nada mais:

(...)
Intersecção (p.46)

Em quinto lugar, encontramos os textos que homenageiam a oralidade, lembrando que quase toda a sua produção poética é um hino à oralidade. A temática anterior, sobre a noite, está em estrita ligação com esta, pois, geralmente, ela, na tradição africana, concretiza-se nocturnamente:
Quando a sombra segrega
o dorso do pranto
o vento suspeito
a ausência da luz
e o **regresso da oralidade**
fazem-se mais cedo

Apego da luz (p.35)

Brando apaga-se pelo apogeu
e pelos pêlos do **gesto verbal**

assim a lua tem vencido
o fundo do fogo
com o signo da língua
quando bem utilizada
a palavra
Signo da língua (p.38)

Embora se diga que toda a poesia é filosófica, em sexto e último lugar, como eixo temático, temos os poemas filosóficos, no sentido de serem mais introspectivos e levarem a aspectos metafísicos. Tal dimensão filosófica está sobretudo no diálogo que resulta dos devaneios poéticos que o sujeito tem sobre os antagonismos dos objectos ou ideias:

A morte e a vida

A morte:
apressa-te a viver
faz tempo que
espero pela minha vez

A vida:

apressa-te a chegar
faz tempo que
o meu mandato terminou
Ciclo de ruminação(p.59)
Primeira raiz do fôlego
A água e a terá

a água diz:
inchar-te-ei de água

ó terra firme
dos corais

a terra diz:
engolir-te-ei
ó água (in)poderosa
dos céus
A miragem que lhe ofereço(61)

Ciclo de ruminação (59), A miragem que lhe ofereço (61), A miragem que lhe ofereço (64),Silêncio (79), Palma da lua (86), Tição para fogo I (87), Reinado (88),Lucidez (96), Tundavala (99), Ferrão (103), Tição para o fogo II (105),Trans(fe\pa)rência(110), Doação(112),Corpo Viril(113),Vastidão do olhar(114),Canto promessa(115) constituem o núcleo do que aqui dessigamos por poemas filosóficos.

0. Consolidação

Mediante os factos expostos, postula-se que a Literatura é uma construção humana e a sua interpretação implica elencar todos os campos categoriais que fundamentem as acções do homem. Será, portanto, a Crítica Literária este espaço de confluência multidisciplinar em que essas ciências solidariamente concorrerão para o mesmo fim: a interpretação da obra literária.

David Capelenguela é um autor cuja poesia se enraíza em culturas milenares. A sua poesia exige mais pesquisas e leituras para uma interpretação que se conceba como verdade filosófica quase completa. A pesquisa a que nos referimos não é apenas bibliográfica, mas sim exploratória, implicando estar no terreno, observar conhecer de perto as práticas culturais dos povos por si eleitos. Entretanto, é preciso deixar claro que a nossa análise, embora incompleta, procurou adentrar essas culturas por via de entrevista ao próprio autor e a pessoas que provieram desses lugares.

1. Referências Bibliográfica

Capelenguela, D. (2012). *Ego do Fogo*. Luanda: Triangularte Editora.
Carvalho, R.D. (2014). *Ondula Savana Branca*. Luanda: Grecima.
Macedo, J. (1980). *Poéticas da Literatura Angolana*. Luanda: INALD.
Maestro, J. G. (2017). *Crítica da Razão Literária. O Materialismo Filosófico como Teoria, Crítica e Dialética da Literatura*. Vigo: Editorial Academia del Hispanismo.

Chapbook by Annette Mbapa "Diva" Ikongo

Annette Mbapa "Diva" Ikongo is a lawyer, poet, and alto singer from Tanzania. She holds a Master's Degree in International Conflict and Security from the University of Kent and lives in Brussels, Belgium. Her literary works have been published in the Best New African Poets 2019 & 2020 Anthologies, Anthology of the Ebrahim Hussein Poetry Prize 2014-2020, and Canto Planetario: Hermandad en la Tierra (Spanish Edition).

Alone with the Others

The forest, it knew me by name.
It clothed me and watched them renounce me.
There I was, covered and exposed.
And there we were, starved, like the ones we left behind.

The land, it held my hand.
My body, counted. My fears, realized.
There I was, hopeful and defeated.
And there we were, cold, like the ones we thought would help us.

The sea, she carried my tears.
My screams, she harmonized to her waves.
My name, she engraved...as she washed my body away.
And there we were, blue, like the sky above us.

Our burning homes, we left behind.
Desperately in search of safe ways to get around.
Hoping someone will offer a helping hand.
A mere statistic we have become.

5 pounds, 8 ounces

I imagined that this was what I'd say to you,
I'd say, Baby, come back later.
Mummy is not ready for a daughter.
I'd say I don't love your father, and I'm really not trying to get any fatter.

I'd say, Baby, come back later.
I drink too much and have nothing to my name.
I'd say I still need to learn the ropes of this game
I'd say, give me 10 more years. I'll be ready then.

I'd say, Baby, come back later.
My business just started taking off.
I'd say, I'm scared, and I can't even tell the difference between a cold and a cough.
How then will I make sure you don't have it rough?

I'd say, Baby, come back later.
This is what I'd say because surely, I know better.
But here you are, baby girl, 5 pounds and 8 ounces.

Birdie

Easy there, Birdie.
Breathe in and breathe out,
There's not much you are missing out.

I see you sticking to your *mama's guns*.
I hear you trying to find your sound.
I can almost feel you constantly losing your mind.

Must be nice,
Cozying up to the ones that *got your back*.
Embrace it, Birdie, but not for long.
Because only when you let go can you start to soar.

Hang in there, Birdie.
Yours is a heart that hopes and a zeal that never stops.
You'll see.
Yours are feathers that were built to shield against any weather.

Tuesday

Tuesday,
You may not know this yet,
But you are my absolute favorite.

Unlike the legendary Friday,
You are not filled with mistakes, I won't regret.
You don't get me overly excited like your mate Saturday.
And you stay clear of 3 am heartaches.

You never seem to be swamped like the frowned-upon Monday.
And you don't have that *'we are almost there'* mood,
that Thursday carries everywhere.

You've left the bittersweet sentiments to Sunday
And you don't bear the halfway mark cast upon Wednesday.

You, Tuesday, are clear as day.
With you, I can truly *carpe diem.*
You are the underdog, dearest.
And, naturally, my absolute favorite.

Car Rides

Car rides..that's the metaphor I use
It's easier, I think.
As soon as we get in, we are all in a rush.
To drive, to get there, to get the wheel moving.

We stop when we have to.
Especially when we encounter red lights.
But we'd rather just drive through
And sometimes we do.

We try and enjoy the journey, it's the best part.
We sing along to songs we don't know.
And throw our hands in the sky,
When the other guy is driving too slow.

We love it!
We also just can't wait to get *'there'.*
And there is a *'there'.*
It's where we are heading.

When we finally open the door,
We are met with the obvious.
What we already know,
But somehow, always seem to ignore.
The end of the car ride.

The moon

Today I saw the moon rising.
Slowly, easing the sun,
For all the work it's done.
One step at a time,
Until there was only twilight.

Today I saw the moon rising,
And I thought to myself,
Like the moon,
We try to shine on ourselves and everyone else.
And most times we do, just not in hot, beautiful rays.

I saw the moon rising,
And reflected on my life.
The sun, the moon, the stars.
It's all light.
Oh! How bright it all shines.
But like the moon, some days we shine a little bit less, I guess.
No, I'm certain.

Writer

I am a writer,
And therefore,
I hope you can understand that to me,
Actions don't speak louder.

By all means,
Act right.
But don't forget to tell *it* to me.
To tell me exactly what you mean.

You see, people say,
Well done is better than well said.
But in my experience,
The tongue can offer better things instead.

So while you linger on in what you do,
And on what makes you true,
Don't forget to be fluent too.

Nimbus

He said, 'I'm grateful to all the men who have left you.'
I said, 'Is that right?'
Here he was, my silver lining.
There I was, the cloud.

I watched as he tried to move us forward.
But like running in my dreams,
I couldn't seem to feel my feet.
There was always a sense of defeat.

And so I rained, as heavily as I could,
And demanded to be misunderstood.
I let him hope for rainbows,
Some nights, I let him have those.
Eventually, I left, and he stayed.

When I see him every morning,
I can't help but wish he had paid attention to the warnings.
Because when my thunder finally comes around,
My lightning will have already torn everything to the ground.

Ahoy!

We are just two boats that set sail,
Unaware that we won't prevail.
Turns out we are carried by different winds,
But there's more we can do than just give in.

We'd rather not, because we are in too deep.
We had a plan, we are determined to keep it.
So it's fine to, once in a while, over this, lose sleep.
It's alright to lower the mainsail and weep.

Darling, we must be okay to change course.
This will give you and me room to steer clear.
It does not mean what lies ahead is assured.
It just means it's better than what was here.

I am convinced this storm will pass someday
And our paths will become clear as day.
Different, but clear nonetheless.
And in our own time, we will set sail again.

Forgive Yourself

Forgive yourself for saying yes when you meant no.
Forgive yourself for the days you play back.
Forgive yourself for the random moments,
That your mind chooses to hold on to. Let them go

Forgive yourself for the mini rock bottoms.
Forgive yourself for what you did, refusing to get back up.
Forgive yourself for allowing everyone else but yourself in.
Forgive yourself for the lies you made yourself believe.

Forgive yourself for playing God.
Forgive yourself for holding on to what you need to let go of.
Forgive yourself for the future you might not have.
Forgive yourself for taking so long to forgive yourself.

C'est Tout?

We have been through hell and back,
And we have nothing to show for that.
Not even memories, not even marks.
Not even a couple of broken hearts.

We are fine, we are fantastic.
We are looking rather charismatic.
We are what people call a lesson learned.
Shaken to the core and though apart, still we stand.

Why then doesn't it feel nice?
Why don't I feel like I've won the prize?
Why is having no pain more painful?
Why would I rather resent you?

This cannot be all, but it is.
Nothing more, nothing less.
Our ending is with such finesse.
It's almost like we weren't there in the first place.

10th November

The way the sky is clear today,
It's as if I didn't spend all I have at the hospital yesterday.
As though I didn't stay up all night,
Receiving phone calls from friends telling me, *'It'll be alright'*

The way the birds are singing this morning,
It's as if I haven't just gotten back from choosing a coffin.
As if my head isn't spinning in circles.
Like the chairs and tents outside my house,
are to my home, the only obstacles.

The way the sun is shining,
So bright.
You'd think I could see the light.
You'd think I can work up an appetite.
You'd think I truly believe in everything I'm trying to believe.

It's a lovely day,
You, my love, died on a
Beautiful day.

The Several Stages of Grief

My neighbour's house is on fire.
Everything is burning to the ground.
Everyone is standing and watching as it all turns to dust.

My neighbor is running towards her house,
Heading for the hot flames.
She must be convinced that there are some things she can save.

My neighbour is shouting at the firefighters,
'*Save it all! Save everything you can*' she screams.
She watches as the smoke thickens.
She pauses for a minute and then rushes to go in,
One last time.

My neighbour is on her knees now.
This must be acceptance.
Her eyes are shut, and she almost fails to get up from the ground.

She does,
And so will another house.

Inner Light

Everything reminds you   of everything,
Even when nothing is the same.
You feel that you keep dancing to the same rhythm,
Don't you worry, someday, the music will change.

You struggle to put your puzzle together,
While all the pieces you'd need   you've gathered.
Something is always missing, you think,
Don't you know, you are the centrepiece.

You worry this is how it will always be.
It can, but it doesn't have to.
Once you realize you can set yourself free,
Then you'll see, it was you that you were chained to.

My dear, it's not about what you let in.
Some of it you can't control.
It is about what you let out.
And not always to everyone else,
But from your very soul.

Hush now, the light is not at the end of   the tunnel.
It's right there with you, it's almost blinding.
One day, it will lead you to what's worth finding.

Situationship

I know that you don't get it when I say,
Let's take this slow.
You think I want you to hold the brakes,
No, my lover... not at all.

How do I say this?
You've said it all.
Somewhere between your hellos and goodnights, I heard your I love you.
And somewhere between my *I'm hungry* and emojis,
I've probably said it too.

How do I say this?
I don't want to get there yet... not now, maybe never.
I want us to stay like this forever,
Not shaken by what's out there.

How do I say this?
I don't want to be shown off by you.
I want to be paraded, in fact proclaimed, loud and clear,
and preferably fluent.
But you know how that will quickly have this ruined.

Go slow, I say

Like this? You ask
More slowly... can you feel that build up?
That's what I want for us, love.

Different Kinds of Heartbreak

There's the kind you cannot control.
Shocker.
Losing a child, seeing someone you love end their life.
Slowly losing the memory of your wife.

There's the kind you saw coming.
Inevitable.
All the late nights adding up.
Ignoring your gut.
Letting go after a long fight.

There's the kind that sneaks up on you.
Unannounced.
Falling for a man you can't have.
Your lipstick smudged in half.
Your plate of rice falling to the ground.

And then there's the kind
You inflict on yourself because you have to.
Intentional.

Ripping yourself apart, because you have to trust
That you will be able to put yourself back together.

Heaven

As I drag my broken wings and dry my unending tears,
I battle with my defeat.
My mind, a sacred grotto of fears.

As I mourn my not-so-lasting peace,
And the unforeseen betrayal of her kiss,
I can't help but imagine a place.
A place I will be in soon.

One where these several bottles of wine,
Will eventually turn to water.
And this burning heart of mine,
Withstand what feels like its slaughter.

A place where these vivid nightmares,
Become beautiful celestial dreams.
And where, this, that feels like torment,
Transfigures into a simple lesson learned.

I have to believe that there is such a place,

A place where this heartache will disappear.
Because if this feels like   death,
Then surely, my heaven is near.

House for Sale

Wrecked and renovated recently.
Empty, enough for you and your baggage.
The rooms are wide and open.
Strong floors, built in the 90s.

It floods now and then.
Sometimes blood. Mostly tears.
Recently equipped with self-repair.
The new owner has nothing to fear.

The neighborhood is vibrant and sincere.
Warm all year round, you will never feel alone.
I must stay, the previous owner died here.
Their soul, despite all my efforts, still lingers on.

Looking for a serious buyer.
It's yours, my whole heart, if you want it.

The In-Between

Oh! How they are frowned upon.
Are you in or are you out?
Go big or go home.
Are you happy about it or upset?

Why though? The in-between can be divine.
Like the mid-section of a bottle of wine.
The 2nd trimester of a soon-to-be mom.
Somewhere between foreplay and culmination.
The event that triggers the rise of a nation.

For some reason, the in-between is left out.
Yes! The sun will rise and it will set.
But it's what happens in between that has us on our feet.
It's the *'I've made it this far, might as well finish'* that enables the leap.

The in-between fades in the background.
Easy to be missed, easy to dismiss.
And yet, we live for the in-between
Don't we?

Locked in Time

He is my love.
The man who *'shines the light'* to search for his flashlight.
The man who wanders into the neighbor's house at night.

He is my friend.
The man who no longer remembers my name.
The man who spends most of his time,
Trying to find the keys in his hand.

He is my husband
The man who leaves the iron in the oven.
The man who recounts yesterday's joke with the same passion.

He is my soulmate
The man who got to travel back in time
The man who though gone,
 Will forever be mine.

Os "novíssimos" e a Poética Escrita de Motivação Oral: transdução das traduções de *Raízes Cantam* e *Pintura dos Ecos:* A palavra (de cada geração) é cara só a vida a compra e a beija, Job Sipitali

Numa altura em que se diz, com todas as certezas, que o Romance, na actualidade, é o género maior; pelo menos em Angola, a poesia continua a ser a forma privilegiada de se usar a palavra como manifestação artística. Podemos provar esse dado lendo manuais de bibliografia geral de autores angolanos, como o trabalho de Tomás Lima Coelho, ou recorrendo à lista de publicações da União dos Escritores Angolanos e das editoras que "resistem" pelo país. Lendo dos primórdios (Maia Ferreira e Cordeiro da Mata) e passando por movimentos como MNIA, o Brigadismo Literário e os actuais movimentos juvenis, saberemos que se têm revelado mais poetas do que prosadores. Neste quadro de "muitos poetas" que resulta, em termos qualitativos, em "pouca poesia pura", passaremos a apresentar autores novos, mas legíveis.

Para o primeiro exercício, elegemos dois autores que vêm marcando o seu espaço e o seu tempo, com todas as dificuldades existentes para se sobreviver num mercado literário carente de leitores. Metodologicamente, actuámos a partir de um quadro teórico, introduzindo um conceito apresentado por Jorge Macedo em *Poéticas da*

Literatura Angolana para caracterização desse tipo de poesia que surge nas obras eleitas e por via de questionamentos pontuais aos autores que,sem questionarem, enviavam os textos de partida em língua bantu.

Raízes Cantam é um poemário da autoria de Job Sipitali publicado em 2017, em Lisboa, pela editora Perfil Criativo e, ainda no mesmo ano, em Benguela: uma estréia auspiciosa, porquanto, teve um impacto imediato no cenário literário nacional, diga-se, não por ter sido publicado inicialmente em Lisboa, senão pela força da sua poética que incorpora elementos da filosofia Ovimbundu num contexto em que, entre a massa juvenil, com excepção do Movimento Litteragris e do que sobrava da Brigada Jovem de Literatura, a "Poesia-Dita", maximizada pelo Movimento Lev'Arte, estava na ordem das apresentações, quer em performances de Palco quer em publicações impressas em quase todo o território nacional. Sobre o impacto do livro, em nota de prefácio, escreve o escritor Gociante Patissa: "A província de Benguela volta a inscrever, com caneta dourada, na história da produção literária angolana, um poemário consistente, «Raízes Cantam», que desponta da segunda década do pós-guerra, cujo marco é o ano de 2010, da qual o autor faz parte". Com efeito, é preciso referir que, essa consistência sobre a qual o prefaciador se refere é verificada nos 47 poemas que compõem um poemário que privilegia, na forma, o verso curto, ainda assim de fundo prosaico por inerência do espaço estético oral, podendo-se sintacticamente subtrair-se orações plenas, agrupadas, na quase generalidade, em tercetos, com raríssimas intromissões de outras categorias de estrofes, em que se reflecte o modo de pensar de um jovem ocimbundu dentro de uma cultura mestiça, como é a angolana.

Pintura dos Ecos, de Ema Nzadi, Prémio Literário António Jacinto 2019, tornada público no mesmo ano em que venceu o saudoso concurso de autores estreantes, aos 17 de Outubro, pelo actual Instituto Nacional das Indústrias Culturais e Criativas, no Museu Nacional de História Natural e apresentada na sua terra natal, Zaire, na Mediateca do Soyo aos 26 de Outubro de 2019, é uma obra que produziu "o seu efeito". Embora se lhe reconheça qualidade considerável, se a compararmos com grande parte das publicações do mesmo género, não foi tão midiatizada como muitos livros; porém, tem feito um percurso interessante, tal como o seu autor que, esporadicamente, vai participando de algumas colectâneas nacionais e internacionais. Trata-se de um poemário composto por 31 poemas que incorporam a memória fluvial e práticas culturais do povo Kongo, que habita na província do Zaire. Provérbios, canções, advinhas, ritos e ritmos que espelham as vivências do povo Kongo são incorporados e retrabalhados no quadro da *agristética* (poética do Litteragris) e do sentido estético particular do autor que, embora se estabeleça numa poética de grupo, integra uma cultura de raiz milenar e busca com várias leituras a autonomia que leva à "singularização", sugerida por Vítor Chklovski em sua conceituação de Arte.

Por Poética de Motivação Oral, Macedo (1986) entende que seria possível considerar uma identidade de fundo e forma, decerto diferenciada quer da poética da literatura oral, quer da poética sentimentalista e retórica, seguida por poetas como Tomás Viera da Cruz, Bessa Victor e outros e ainda por aquela que se pode considerar por poética conceitualista de protesto que tem em Agostinho Neto um dos seus maiores adeptos. Macedo (1986, p.47), ao conceber o conceito de "Poética Escrita de Motivação Oral", estaria a pensar sobretudo na poesia que sobrevivia da "tónica coloquial" envolvendo "um nível de deslocação de uma menos-prosa e por vezes a igualando em parte"e, consequentemente, em autores como Viriato da Cruz, Aires de Almeida Santos, entre vários, embora tal conceito nos dê a possibilidade de analisar as obras de Job Sipitali e de Ema Nzadi que incorporando tecidos da literatura oral em suas poéticas, dissolvem-nos ao ponto de os menos atentos verem passar essas marcas como meros actos de criatividade. Com efeito, inscrevemos-lhes nessa poética porque é evidente a pretensão de os seus autores firmarem as suas culturas nas suas obras, quer em actos de criação quer em conversas de bastidores. Job Sipitali, em conversa mantida através do *Facebook*, confidenciou-nos ser um poeta que mais considera a Literatura Oral do que qualquer outra coisa e de como a sua vivência rural com o modo de vida filosófica dos mais velhos constituíram-se como o eixo crucial para a construção da sua poesia, revelando um mundo filosófico-transcendental com o cunho dos princípios da ancestralidade, onde primeiro se busca a filosofia ancestral e só depois Suku(Deus). Com outras palavras, Ema Nzadi admitiu-nos mover-se dentro dessa mentalidade referida pelo seu companheiro de arte e de movimento, tendo igualmente nos ajudado a resolver um enigma em relação à produção de ambos, reafirmada também por Job Sipitali. Ambos extraem da oralidade (filosofia) e da realidade social angolana de forma geral (as temáticas) a matéria que manipulam através das suas ideoestéticas. Ema Nzadi refere que não escreve na forma original para dar tonalidades mais literárias, não se conforta só com essas formas, constrói outras imagens para simbolizar o natural e acredita que a natureza merece esse exercício.

Em face do que se disse no parágrafo anterior, no poema de Job Sipitali intitulado "No Ventre do Silêncio Materno" só o verso *Usar a palavra é procurar a perfeição* (*Okukwata ondaka okuvandja elipwo em umbundu*) se inscreve originalmente na lista de provérbios ovimbundu, o resto é criação:

Se a caneta não peca, é porque o tempo é perfeito.| Se peca, é porque o tempo se corrompeu.|Se não se corrompeu, é porque o silêncio a usou.| Usar a palavra é procurar a perfeição.| Se a tinta usa o papel, é porque se comprometeu a ser.| Belo é o que é dito no silêncio.| Oh! Minha mãe, no silêncio ventral| está seu nome com a geração...| Pois, tudo é vital p'ra quem em vós espera. (Sipitali, 2017, p.52)

Parece-nos que a incorporação de textos orais em *Raízes Cantam* obedece praticamente a mesma ordem, funcionando ora como mote para a construção de um poema ora como uma memória que vem reforçar o exercício poético-filosófico onde, geralmente, a dimensão dialéctica assume a sua essência de objecção como no poema "O Mito da Cor", em que o provérbio *Iko likovonga ovilelembia* (A fogueira evoca os espíritos) encontra a sua expressão antagônica nos dois versos seguintes :

...O MITO DA COR...| Toma-se a cor pela palavra.|A garganta enriquece-se

*de mitos nocturnos./A fogueira evoca os espíritos,|**enquanto a lenha se prolonga|esperando a verdade.**| Mente quem conhece a história do pescador de palavras./E eu sou balaio que se estende ao silêncio.* (Sipitali, 2017, p.15)

Em Ema Nzadi, por vezes, a incorporação desses elementos da oralidade (provérbio, advinha, etc.) implica uma dissolução da estrutura linguística, uma espécie de reinterpretação pessoal, que o leva a sair directamente do texto de partida (Kikongo) para o universo da poesia escrita em língua portuguesa. Assim, "Longoka e ngangu, kala ye ngangu zaku" salta da sua tradução literal "Para adquirir um conhecimento, é preciso que tenhas o seu próprio conhecimento" para,

para terra dos Bantu/um grito certo de olhar/desta voz perdida D sopros ruídos/caminhar vós elefantes do sol(...)/para terra dos pássaros mil espelhos a vida transforma/os guinchos trombetas evoquem sombras... caminhemos/(N)OSSO (Nzadi, 2019, p.42)

O texto aponta para a necessidade de valorização daquilo que, de forma natural, deveria causar sentimento de pertença e que nunca se deveria perder: a cultura, as línguas,em suma, a terra e tudo o que nela há. Em virtude disso, para acentuar a força do seu enunciado, Ema Nzadi coloca o monema "N" dentro de parênteses para se focar no resto da estrutura que consagra o lexema "OSSO" como símbolo de força, aquilo que sustenta, e no seu sentido místico, se compreendermos o espaço estético como o lugar onde o artífice forja a sua arte e este mergulha numa religiosidade que opera com vários instrumentos entre eles o "osso" que também aponta para o que sobra do corpo físico, entre outras coisas. Essa forma de tradução de Ema Nzadi, que dilui os sentidos textuais num novo corpus (poético), vê-se também em "In digna Ação":

Fazer do tempo/sono secular/se não vibrarem braços/terra sobre a massa das nuvens/serão deuses a ressurgirem/flutuando com os olhos/na noite fazendo tempo/IN DIGNA AÇÃO (Nzadi, 2019, p.26)

O poema resulta do provérbio de um Kikongo (Nzila a moyo ke lekelwangako o kuntuala, mpasi wa wana edivene) que o poeta teve dificuldade em traduzir literalmente em português. Interpretando o texto, explica que o provérbio se revela como uma chamada de atenção com veios de indignação e diz que não há tempo oportuno para se fazer alguma coisa. Todos os tempos valem dependendo da capacidade de execução, porque, quando se espera o tempo oportuno, pode-se encontrar malícia.

A recorrência à oralidade não pressupõe alheamento. As questões sociais mais latentes que afligem o país não são deixadas de lado por esses jovens poetas. Ema Nzadi, em "Kimbemba" (sonhei fome), apropria-se de um canto proverbial entoado geralmente por ocasião da morte de uma entidade cultural, um "Kulumbundu" (representante máximo da família) ou um "Ntinu" (rei de uma tribo):
britas de nuvens/mãos com bares sindrómicas /por corpo nuvens falam álcool/lama dos verbos cheios de promessas/de paraquedas dez 100 estrelas/a arma é o vento, nem produz!/ falam-me os gritos kimbemba/pelo menos morra eu em cantos/saudades deixarei/fome também/deixa/errei/KIMBEMBA(SONHEI SEM FOME). (Nzadi, 2019, p.38)

Mbemba é uma ave que está sempre no ar e é vista como um símbolo importante. Quando aterra em algum lugar é porque vai buscar alguma coisa. Dela descende Kimbemba, a morte de entidades importantes, equiparadas à ave que, quando morrem, levam tudo: sabedoria, poder e protecção. Em contramão, Sipitali, em jeito de máximas, tendo como ponto de partida o provérbio "ohū otchili tch'utima", que significa "O silêncio é uma irracionalidade certa", último verso do poema abaixo descrito, leva-nos a questionar o sentido da missão que cada um de nós traz consigo, repudia a cobardia que

impede o progresso da liberdade de expressão e convoca para a palavra incinerada:
MISSÃO...| *O* ex professo | *Carrega consigo* | *O nacionalismo aurido.* / *O compreensivo* | *Segue o anel*| *que o Mundo deve.* / *Deve a palavra incinerada* / *nas espreguiçadeiras do verbo.*| *O silêncio é uma irracionalidade certa.* p.17

Job Sipitali, em *Raízes Cantam*, e Ema Nzadi, em *Pintura dos Ecos*, produzem uma poesia que se distancia qualitativamente da maioria dos seus símiles porque, para além de cultivarem hábitos de leitura, têm a seu favor uma dupla vivência e não ignoram nenhuma delas: o campo, onde se conservam saberes milenares ignorados por uma maioria, e a escola de matriz ocidental, da qual extraem apenas o necessário para as suas produções. Para além dos poemários, tivemos contacto com obras no prelo e podemos afirmar, mesmo com a segurança de um Crítico em construção, que ambos vêm para marcar a história da poesia angolana.
Macedo,J.(1986). *Poéticas Na Literatura Angolana*. Luanda:INALD.
Nzadi,E.(2019). *Pinturas dos Ecos*. Luanda:INIC.
Sipitali, J.(2017*)*. *Raízes Cantam*.Lisboa:Perfil Criativo.

Nature sings by Obinna Chilekezi

Obinna Chilekezi was born in Diobu Port Harcourt, Rivers State, Nigeria, has a PhD in enterpreneurship. He is a Chartered Insurance Practitioner and has written many books on Insurance, of which one of them won the African Insurance Organisation Book Award in 2016. He started writing poems at an early age. His poems have appeared in Newspapers and journals like Daily Times, Daily Trust, Times International, Rake, ANA Review, Better Than Starbucks, Borderless Journal, Verse-Virtual Pandemic Poems 2020, Inakitto – The Nalubaale Review Literary Magazine, Round Robin by Poetry Society of Indiana, Cajun Muth Press. His poems have been published in anthologies like Wahun 2, Twenty Nigerian Writers (ANA Lagos): For Ken, For Nigeria (E. C. Osondu): New Voices. He has published six collections of poems among which are Songs of a Stranger in the Smiling Coast, My Gambian and other poems, Moonlight songs.

Movement song

The tight curls of life, have I studied, watching it
Moves in just nature one way of life

Then I paused and waited, again and again
And this rain falls, falls and falls abnormally
Watching the River Gambia emptying its water into the ocean

My age reversed backward
And father that early sermon spoke
Of why I should know who I am
Ah father where is he now?
Living just in my dream
Beyond anger of my father

Forward to move I also must
Waiting till the time of the pollen fall
Without goodbyes.

Good morning birds

Kuku ble kuku, kuku ble kuku
It is morning, and fresh bird songs
Flow across that cold early morn

The birds twit and sing,
Walking down to the window,
Behold two beautiful birds singing
And I obliged them with a good morning too

For love's sake

I traverse the land, the sea and the air
And here am I at the doorstep of your heart
Knocking,
While I watch this lonely bird perched at the tip of the grass,

Sad
I have seen such corrosive kiss of love
And healing touch, too, of morning love

The lone bird perched at the tip of the leaf

With mouthful of morning curses of dejection
But in wait, waiting for consoling touch of love

Here am I too
Knocking on the heart of Venus
For it is only the mirror that knows all that it had seen

The bleeding heart is like a sunless day, it has no smile

Yet it's raining outside
Heavy rains out there and you are in the rain
Dancing in the rain, with sparkling smiles of the sun

A healing wind touches the wings of the lone bird
Perching at the tip of the leave, tip of love

If it heals you, it will heal me too

Wake up and love
With nourishing love for all
Freeing us of shackles of bitter years gone

Rainbow

stars closed up in their sockets, dimmed
no bird's singsong still
and distressed stone terrac winds
fanning downward and upward

after that heated noon
the rains bathe the sky
and the sky smiles
in gratitude

a rainbow
was born

Nightingale

Sweet melodic bird
immortal in my mind
Songs
sweetly orchestrated in eardrums
at the fragrant bushpart behind

whilst silver moon sailing and smiling

The song burst from a tree's hand:
chook, chook, chook...
pio, pioo, pioo, ...
all in a crescendo chucking
of night's notes of mellow
aploms: o' my apotheosis
your voice
rendered me aphasia
wish i, o' wish, wish
i could envelope your songs
in an earthen pot container forever
where when i need it:
those songs of a lover
crying out its heart for more love:
i
itys, itys, itys ...

O' nightingale
sing more songs of love, for
sorrowed smitten souls to mend
whose hopes had been Sapped
but, theirs: persistent love
twinkling, twinkling ever as a star

Harmattan Dawn

Confusing, this dawn again
yes, the day ought to have broken by now
dark traps everywhere
traps hidden in the wet grass
as drops of dew scatter
and glisten the dark

Moment later
the chilled sunlight appears with it –
fresh songs of a new day
and raw yolky sound of birdsongs, everywhere

The dawn is at our feet again
Wake as fast as an antelope
for fear of the day's lion ahead

Dawn

The day crawls to break
As drops of dews scatter the ground with mist
Cold, yet Cockerel struggling to crow
This is dawn, chilling dawn light
Creeps into the room through the window
Of the day, of wet grasses

With traps of hidden
Fear of the new day walking into dusk

Wake up, I heard, it is morning
Stinging pains of dawn sting on me
As fresh silence strikes me at the face
Thank God it's dawn, Good morning dawn
So says the raw sounds of birdsongs
As I struggle to face the day today.
2005

Your card arrived

The flowerily card arrived
With lipstick marks
Telegraphing your roly-poly
Arousing thoughts, shared thoughts
with you
Moonlighting together
The hibiscus drawn card, red like rose
Arrived like a thief

It brings with it surprises, of silent seeking
In this unexpected time, just like
A cream creaming against jagged cracks
With its bleaching effects on our stained spot

An escape from

at times we have to
leave the pay-seat of boredom
escape from ourselves for a while

just to the beach I dashed
leaving behind the thorns of work,
the pages of work to attend

sitting on the pay-seat
I stopped listening to music
and only to the corrosive voice of mine

here at the beach, all alone, I sat
as gust of wind slammed my face
with a clap of sound, and of peace

carefully I listen and listen
to the sweet sounds of drifting sand
I listen to the tiny whispering wind
in the dunes' grasses

oh how it feels to be on your own

free, in sweet presence of nature
just away from the pay-seat

Half of the yellow sun

The sun rises
and set at dawn
it dimmed across
these depleted bunkers of mind
and it rises again

half a yellow sun
at dawn
in the minds of urchins
who did not witnessed the last
half a yellow sun
with its score strife effects

the quest for half a yellow sun
this time around, the aftermath of
a mapped agenda from unlearnt lesson of history

The melt down

Another dusk, economic dusk,
Brother here we are again,
The locusts come visiting,
In the midst of a market meltdown.

A time like this,
Is not a time for blame games,

A time like this,
Requires tons of courage.

Brother!
Set aside your pride, roll up your sleeves,

This labour will be faced by all,
Convict or not.

Frustrated people

Swampy life,
After a barren afternoon,
Life went grey,
Its penis amputated,
By this gibbering society.

Frustrated lot,
Dressed in sorrow and self-pity,
Wait at the roadside,
For hope to stop by,
As the sun, drunk with tears and sweats
Staggers home.

As we wait,
for this hope that will never stop by
I recall the Lord's prayer,
Mumbled 'Give us this day,
Our daily bread', as dusk
Spread its shadow, over our dreams.

Walking away from bygone of you

Adventures in the wild wind life
As I walked my shadow down the lonely road,
A blackbird, perching on the tendrils of
A garden lilac, sang a tune for one.
Dusk hung around the valley,
Rehearsing verses of silence.

Yes, like Simeon
I too have seen the Lord
And I wait at the dawn gate of my fortune ...
There're good fortunes
Indeed at dawn.
I walked forward silently
Over any hill, mountain and valley
Forward in silence walk i
Away from these bygone
Adventures of a youth

Economic meltdown

The owl is out in the market
Swarm of locusts everywhere
The market has burnt down
To ashes and loud cries of hunger
In mentholated dusting powdered pains.

With the rest, I staggered along
As the delusive gravitating scorn
Of scorn of singsongs aloud abound
From all official quarters

I, too have seen, the night breaking
Into the full, fresh fragrant morning
And the night of doom over

Yes, not under this present regime
But I know, my pain has an end

For a new dawn

As night gives
Way to morning
The chrysalis
A butterfly
My dream dawn
To great things
Who knows?

This chrysalis
At break of morning
A new hope beginning

My dawn, my dream
My chrysalis, my butterfly

It is a new day, a new hope to behold.

Umunama

Give me my homeland's lakes and streams;
Her many charms display
Before my homesick, lonesome eyes
When I am away

- Evelyn Preston Mclean

Not that I would love not to live in you
because of the darkness, the red sandy rough roads,
the screams of insects and crickets;
sights of old women laboring
with heavy basketful
sights of stalls, shops, kiosks –
the Orieukwu coming to life only at evening fall.
Groansof hunger, and tattered children; yes,
quick reference to our dreamed differed rural setting.

Yet I love you, Umunama
I love your fireflies
littering nightfall as starry phantasm
I love your moonlight children's songs,
yet familiar with our jungle-cities' urchins in my abode
I love your care-for-one-another lifestyle
I love the landscapes, Ala'ku's rickety landscape
of our myth-lore riverbed without water;
but valleys unerected as peaks
like a granny burst
I love you, woman
to you, I'd come after this prodigal flight
for spiritual refurbishment
1990

Together as sky

our views differ ...

as the sun from the moon
but the linearity of love
and desire solves the quadratic equation

we are like the Niger and Benue
always separately on a move
meeting at a confluence

come love, come
for our correlation coefficient
of our linear existence is love

just as that of moon and stars ...

we'll then be together
me and you
you and me
together as one

Poem of dawn at dawn

the morning star still shines
and the earth dims
as men strip to their beddings
like a swarm of tired bees

dawn
time of mind's harvest
when head is still fresh
when head still fresh
from restive sleep
while men of underworld operate
under darkness cover

I write this poem of dawn
at dawn
before the strips of the sky
'd fall on me from high
With the day's burning effect

Rejection

it
may come
in different cloths

it may come
like a dream
half dreamt

it may come
live a dove descending
with darkly news

like a gale of fire
heating the house and its hold
it may come

in the song
unsung
it may come like fierce
wild wind, not to be
grasped or weighed

rejection enwombed
in dreams
never dreamt

rejection in everyday existence
and by you, it is
that pain in me which never
hurt my soul

Mmap New African Poets Series

If you have enjoyed *AFRICAN POETRY ANTHOLOGY: Chapbooks, Vol 1* consider these other fine books in the **Mmap New African Poets Series** from *Mwanaka Media and Publishing:*

I Threw a Star in a Wine Glass by Fethi Sassi
Best New African Poets 2017 Anthology by Tendai R Mwanaka and Daniel Da Purificacao
Logbook Written by a Drifter by Tendai Rinos Mwanaka
Mad Bob Republic: Bloodlines, Bile and a Crying Child by Tendai Rinos Mwanaka
Zimbolicious Poetry Vol 1 by Tendai R Mwanaka and Edward Dzonze
Zimbolicious Poetry Vol 2 by Tendai R Mwanaka and Edward Dzonze
Zimbolicious: An Anthology of Zimbabwean Literature and Arts, Vol 3 by Tendai Mwanaka
Under The Steel Yoke by Jabulani Mzinyathi
Fly in a Beehive by Thato Tshukudu
Bounding for Light by Richard Mbuthia
Sentiments by Jackson Matimba
Best New African Poets 2018 Anthology by Tendai R Mwanaka and Nsah Mala
Words That Matter by Gerry Sikazwe

The Ungendered by Delia Watterson
Ghetto Symphony by Mandla Mavolwane
Sky for a Foreign Bird by Fethi Sassi
A Portrait of Defiance by Tendai Rinos Mwanaka
Zimbolicious: An Anthology of Zimbabwean Literature and Arts, Vol 4 by Tendai Mwanaka and Jabulani Mzinyathi
When Escape Becomes the only Lover by Tendai R Mwanaka
وَالغَمَام...ويَسـهَرُ اللَّيلُ عَلَى شَفَتي by Fethi Sassi
A Letter to the President by Mbizo Chirasha
This is not a poem by Richard Inya
Pressed flowers by John Eppel
Righteous Indignation by Jabulani Mzinyathi:
Blooming Cactus by Mikateko Mbambo
Rhythm of Life by Olivia Ngozi Osouha
Travellers Gather Dust and Lust by Gabriel Awuah Mainoo
Chitungwiza Mushamukuru: An Anthology from Zimbabwe's Biggest Ghetto Town by Tendai Rinos Mwanaka
Zimbolicious: An Anthology of Zimbabwean Literature and Arts, Vol 5 by Tendai Mwanaka
Because Sadness is Beautiful? by Tanaka Chidora
Of Fresh Bloom and Smoke by Abigail George
Shades of Black by Edward Dzonze

Best New African Poets 2020 Anthology by Tendai Rinos Mwanaka, Lorna Telma Zita and Balddine Moussa
This Body is an Empty Vessel by Beaton Galafa
Between Places by Tendai Rinos Mwanaka
Best New African Poets 2021 Anthology by Tendai Rinos Mwanaka, Lorna Telma Zita and Balddine Moussa
Zimbolicious: An Anthology of Zimbabwean Literature and Arts, Vol 6 by Tendai Mwanaka and Chenjerai Mhondera
A Matter of Inclusion by Chad Norman
Keeping the Sun Secret by Mariel Awendit
سِجلٌّ مَكتُوبٌ لتَائه □ by Tendai Rinos Mwanaka
Ghetto Blues by Tendai Rinos Mwanaka
Zimbolicious: An Anthology of Zimbabwean Literature and Arts, Vol 7 by Tendai Rinos Mwanaka and Tanaka Chidora
Best New African Poets 2022 Anthology by Tendai Rinos Mwanaka and Helder Simbad
Dark Lines of History by Sithembele Isaac Xhegwana
a sky is falling by Nica Cornell
Death of a Statue by Samuel Chuma
Along the way by Jabulani Mzinyathi
Strides of Hope by Tawanda Chigavazira
Young Galaxies by Abigail George
Coming of Age by Gift Sakirai

Mother's Kitchen and Other Places by Antreka. M. Tladi
Best New African Poets 2023 Anthology by Tendai Rinos Mwanaka, Helder Simbad and Gerald Mpesse
Zimbolicious Anthology Vol 8 by Tendai Rinos Mwanaka and Mathew T Chikono
Broken Maps by Riak Marial Riak
Formless by Raïs Neza Boneza
Of poets, gods, ghosts. Irritants and storytellers by Tendai Rinos Mwanaka
Ethiopian Aliens by Clersidia Nzorozwa
In The Inferno by Jabulani Mzinyathi
Who Told You To Be God by Mariel Awendit
Nobody Loves Me by Abigail
The Stories of Stories by Nkwazi Mhango
Nhorido by Siphosami Ndlovu and Tinashe Chikumbo
Best New African Poets 10th Anniversary: Selected English African Poets by Tendai Rinos Mwanaka
Best New African Poets 10th Anniversary: Interviews and Reviews of African Poets by Tendai Rinos Mwanaka
Best New African Poets 10th Anniversary: African Languages and Collaborations by Tendai Rinos Mwanaka
Penetration by Tapuwa, Tremor Mapaike
ANTOLOGIA DOS MELHORES "NOVOS" POETAS AFRICANOS 10º Aniversário: Poetas

Africanos Da Língua Portuguesa Selecionados by Lorna Telma Zita and Tendai Rinos Mwanaka
ABRACADABRA, by Olivia Ngozi Osuoha
DES MEILLEURS "NOUVEAUX" POÈTES AFRICAINS
10 Anniversaire : Poètes africains d'expression française by Geraldin Mpesse and Tendai Rinos Mwanaka
Taurai Amai by Cosmas Tasvika Manhanhanha
Nhemeramutupo by Oscar Gwiriri
Ntombentle: Selected Poems by Sithembele Isaac Xhegwana
Juices Of The Forbidden Fruit by Tapuwa Tremor Mapaike

www.ingramcontent.com/pod-product-compliance
Lightning Source LLC
Chambersburg PA
CBHW052046220426
43663CB00012B/2463